What's in Ted's Wallet?
The Newly Revealed
T206 Baseball Card Collection
Of Thomas Edison's Youngest Son

J.B. Manheim & Lawrence Knorr

SUNBURY
PRESS ®

Mechanicsburg, PA USA

Published by Sunbury Press, Inc.
Mechanicsburg, PA USA

SUNBURY
PRESS ®

www.sunburypress.com

For information about special discounts for bulk purchases, please contact Sunbury Press Orders Dept. at (855) 338-8359 or orders@sunburypress.com.

To request one of our authors for speaking engagements or book signings, please contact Sunbury Press Publicity Dept. at publicity@sunburypress.com.

FIRST SUNBURY PRESS EDITION: April 2024

Set in Adobe Garamond Pro | Interior design by Crystal Devine | Cover by Lawrence Knorr | Edited by John Jordan.

Publisher's Cataloging-in-Publication Data
Names: Manheim, J.B., author | Knorr, Lawrence, author.
Title: What's in Ted's wallet : the newly revealed T206 baseball card collection of Thomas Edison's youngest son / J.B. Manheim & Lawrence Knorr.
Description: First trade paperback edition. | Mechanicsburg, PA : Sunbury Press, 2024.
Summary: For a few months in 1909–1910, Thomas Edison's youngest son, Ted, collected several dozen T206 baseball cards, which he carried around in a well-worn wallet. The authors came across these cards in the archive of the Thomas Edison National Historical Park. What's In Ted's Wallet? gives readers a look at this important collection and places it in context.
Identifiers: ISBN : 979-8-88819-218-4 (paperback) | ISBN : 979-8-88819-219-1 (ePub).
Subjects: ANTIQUES & COLLECTIBLES / Sports Cards / Baseball | BIOGRAPHY & AUTOBIOGRAPHY / Rich & Famous | SPORTS & RECREATION / Baseball / History.

Designed in the USA
0 1 1 2 3 5 8 13 21 34 55

For the Love of Books!

Cover: The photograph of Theodore Edison was found online April 12, 2024, at https://npgallery.nps.gov/AssetDetail/f17f2fe3-13ee-4d25-a438-af8b85e70fab#. Courtesy of the National Park Service.

Contents

Thomas Edison and Baseball

I don't believe you can find a more ardent follower of baseball than myself, as a day seldom passes when I do not read the sporting pages of the newspapers. In this way I keep close tab on the two major leagues and there was one time when I could name the players of every club in both leagues.[1]

THOSE WORDS, penned by Thomas Edison in a feature article he wrote for the *Palm Beach Post* in 1927, captured a little-known side of the great inventor.

By 1927, Edison and his wife Mina had been spending part of every winter at a getaway estate in Fort Myers, Florida, that the couple shared with Henry Ford and his wife Clara. Also in Fort Myers for a part of the winter beginning in 1925 were Connie Mack and his Philadelphia Athletics baseball club, who held their annual spring training at the nearby Terry Park Ballfield, which had been designed by Mack and built by a local entrepreneur. Edison visited the A's practice sessions in at least two of those years, 1926 and 1927, where he became friends with Mack and, when he joined the club in 1927, with Ty Cobb. The picture on the next page depicts the trio in 1927.

---

1. Excerpted from Thomas A. Edison, "Baseball Greatest Game, Says Edison: Inventor Lauds Cobb as Fine Manhood Type, Urges Youths to Follow," *The Palm Beach Post*, February 23, 1927, p. 2.

Ty Cobb, Thomas Edison, and Connie Mack[2]

Though a man of eighty years at the time, Edison still enjoyed playing the game as well as watching it, and in one instance, borrowed a bat from Al Simmons, the team's young slugger, and challenged Cobb to pitch to him while Mack played catcher. There are various renderings of this story, including those in which Edison hit a line drive off Cobb's shoulder, knocking him down while some nearby reporters shouted, "Sign him up!"[3] Afterward, Edison invited the entire team to visit Seminole Lodge, his nearby home, for lunch, where he handed out cigars to each man.

2. The photo showing Edison with Ty Cobb and Connie Mack at the Fort Myers ballpark, taken March 7, 1927, is in the National Park Service archive and was found online June 4, 2023, at https://npgallery.nps.gov/EDIS/AssetDetail/2a2ba1bfedc440889b09dd77e00576d4. Courtesy National Park Service.

3. See Dan Holmes, "When Ty Cobb and Thomas Edison met in spring training," January 15, 2018, found online May 28, 2023, at https://www.vintagedetroit.com/ty-cobb-thomas-edison-met-spring-training/; the Edison and Ford Winter Estates Blog entry, "Baseball at Terry Park – From Edison to Today," found online May 28, 2023, at https://www.edisonfordwinterestates.org/baseball-at-terry-park-from-edison-to-today/; and Hughie Jennings, "Thomas Edison Lights Up Ty Cobb," found online May 28, 2023, at https://hughiejennings.com/the-ee-yah-blog/f/thomas-edison-lights-up-ty-cobb.

When he noticed that everyone was putting the stogies in their pockets rather than smoking them, Edison asked the reason. Told that they were regarded as souvenirs of the visit, he sent for more cigars so they could be enjoyed as intended. At that point, Mina Edison intervened to announce that punch was being served.[4]

In fact, Edison's connections to baseball went far deeper. As early as 1885, Edison had been approached by a Canadian entrepreneur who sought to collaborate with him to develop incandescent lighting for baseball fields to permit the playing of games at night.[5] There is no evidence that such an arrangement was ever consummated, though at least one interpretation of the photo above holds that this was the very subject that Edison, shown looking skyward, was discussing with Mack and Cobb some forty years later. In 1898, Edison's motion picture company produced the very first baseball film, *The Ball Game*, which depicts a player in a Newark, New Jersey, uniform running to first base with a grandstand in the background.[6] That player has subsequently been identified as future western adventure author Zane Grey, who was a talented ballplayer in his youth. The following year, 1899, Edison produced another short film, *Casey at the Bat*, which was shot on the lawn of his Glenmont estate.[7]

Gray had a baseball-related side story of his own. In 1909, he published a widely read baseball novel, *The Short-Stop*, based on his boyhood love of the game. The success of that book led him to begin a series of young adult books featuring a character named Ken Ward. The second book in this series, *The Young Pitcher*, published in 1911, was another baseball title. During this same period, he produced a series of baseball short stories that were published in various magazines; these were collected and published in 1920 in *The Redheaded Outfield and Other*

4. This account was provided by Alexandra Edwards, Marketing and Public Relations Coordinator for the Edison and Ford Winter Estates. Personal correspondence with the author.

5. This letter, which resembles in appearance a telegraph, was found online, May 27, 2023, at https://edisondigital.rutgers.edu/iiif/2/222823/full/749,/0/default.jpg and https://edisondigital.rutgers.edu/iiif/2/222824/full/722,/0/default.jpg. Provided by the Thomas A. Edison Papers at Rutgers University.

6. Edison Studios produced "The Ball Park," a fifty-second-long clip showing a baseball game featuring a team from Newark, in 1888. The film, available through the Library of Congress, was found online May 27, 2023, at https://www.loc.gov/item/00563587/.

7. See John Thorn, "Early Baseball Film," *Medium*, August 22, 2022, found online March 12, 2024, at https://ourgame.mlblogs.com/early-baseball-film-3ffab5c6d24a.

Stories.[8] Ted was born in the same year Gray appeared in Edison's film, so clearly, no connection between the two would have been established at that time. However, it is entirely likely that Ted would have viewed *The Ball Game*, perhaps more than once, during his boyhood, and since Grey would have emerged during that time as a prominent writer, it is also quite possible his father told him of the connection.

Beginning in 1912, the Edison Company in West Orange sponsored a series of annual Field Day events which always included an interdepartmental baseball contest. Edison is pictured here at about age sixty-five in an old snapshot from the first of these events, in 1912, pitching to an actual batter. The photo was altered at the time to show the supposed path of the baseball and the bat.

Edison on the Mound, 1912[9]

8. John Thorn, "Zane Grey's 'The Young Pitcher,' an Odd Baseball Novel," found online April 4, 2024, at https://ourgame.mlblogs.com/zane-greys-the-young-pitcher-an-odd-baseball-novel-e249dcc723a5.

9. The snapshot of Edison pitching to a live batter, taken July 16, 1912, is in the National Park Service archive and was found online June 4, 2023, at https://www.nps.gov/npgallery/AssetDetail/cd9889fd-0db4-4ece-8ce5-127b8d7b9422. Courtesy National Park Service.

Edison was, of course, a local celebrity, so it should not be surprising that the Newark newspaper wrote up this event.

Stepping on the pitching slab with the air and grace of a Marquard or a Johnson, Edison wound up in true league style and shot the ball across the centre of the plate for a clean strike. The proud catcher stationed behind the plate said that Mr. Edison had speed to burn. He also used a curve ball that nearly worked havoc with the receiver, who was expecting a slow, straight one.[10]

Various Edison companies sponsored semi-professional teams that played in the industrial leagues that were prevalent early in the twentieth

century. One of these teams was the Brooklyn Edisons, pictured here in 1909.

10. "Edison Makes Merry at Picnic: 'Wizard' Takes Holiday and Romps and Plays with Employees," *Newark Star-Eagle*, July 17, 1912, p. 4.

The 1909 Brooklyn Edison[11]

After a false start the year before, funded in part by Mr. Edison himself, in 1914, the Edison Club of Orange, New Jersey, began to field its own team made up of employees of the Edison Works.[12] Funding the squad was a challenge, as it received only limited support from the company itself. So, before the very first game that year, the team held a fund-raising banquet at which a feature event was the premier of still more short baseball films produced by Edison, this time featuring New York Giants Manager John J. McGraw relating a series of humorous and other baseball stories.[13]

Though no photographs of the Edison Baseball Club from that earliest period are available, we do know that the team continued to play well into the 1920s and that Edison himself continued his interest. Both facts are captured in the photograph below, a "typical" team photo of that and later eras, except that this one shows the inventor himself as the central figure.

---

11. The photo of the 1909 Brooklyn Edisons was found online May 27, 2023, at http://www.covehurst.net/ddyte/brooklyn/semipro_parks.html.

12. Letter from Clarence Hayes, team president and manager, to Ernest Berggren, Edison Company head accountant, dated March 27, 1914. Courtesy of the Thomas Edison NHP archives.

13. "J. J. McGraw in Movies at Edison Ball Club's Affair," *Newark Evening Star*, January 28, 1914, 4.

The Edison Baseball Club[14]

At least two Brooklyn baseball fields of that early period were named after the famous inventor. From 1907 onward, Brooklyn Edison company teams, known variously as Ampere Athletic Club, the Edisons, or the Voltas, played in one such park, known as Edison Field I, located at an area known as Visitation Oval or Visitation Park. Another location, at Brooklyn's Washington Park, was known for a time in the 1920s as Edison Field II. And by 1932 there was yet another eponymous field, Edison Field III, this one in Astoria, Queens.[15] But one of Edison's more noteworthy contributions to baseball facilities doesn't bear his name at all. Though little noted today, one of the inventor's most significant creations was an effective new production process for what is known as Portland cement, a mixture of limestone, clay, and gypsum that provides for especially strong bonding. Some forty-five thousand barrels of the stuff were used in 1922

14. This team photo, dated circa the 1920s, was found online July 9, 2023, at https://www.rswliving.com/events/199743/vintage-baseball-game-at-terry-park/. The photo was taken by Lewis Lueder, Edison's official photographer, when he was an employee of Thomas A. Edison, Inc., later McGraw-Edison. McGraw-Edison transferred copyright of all historical materials created by the company or its employees, including this photo, to the United States government, i.e., to the public domain. The authors have been unable to locate the original of the photo.

15. See "Brooklyn's Semipro Fields," found online March 12, 2024, at http://www.covehurst.net/ddyte/brooklyn/semipro_parks.html.

in the building of the first Yankee Stadium. It may have been the House that Ruth Built, but it was built with Edison Portland Cement.

Oddly enough, the idea to use Edison Portland Cement in stadium construction may have occurred first, not in the Bronx with Yankee Stadium, but fully ten years earlier in Brooklyn with Ebbetts Field. Or so the *Brooklyn Eagle* would have had its readers believe. In a 1912 article headlined "Edison at Work on Ebbetts Field," the paper reported:

> Several improvements that the architect overlooked will be poured in with the [special quick-drying Edison] concrete. These will include electric fans under every seat to keep the human fans cool when the umpire loses his mind. There will be taps every two feet, which, on the pressure of a button, will give forth enthusiasm and joy in unlimited quantities.
>
> The diamond, Mr. Edison says, will be inlaid with electric "ginger wires" and the simple turning of a switch will cause even the laziest player to take some interest when the game seems hopelessly lost.

As far-sighted as these improvements might have been—even going so far as to add a buzz to the game—it is worth noting that the article in question was published in the newspaper's April 1 edition.[16]

Edison saw baseball as "the greatest of American games," one he tended to view in the moralistic terms common to his era. Interestingly, he saw Ty Cobb not as the villain of the game portrayed by his teammates and so many others but as a paragon of clean living, "one of the cleanest the game has ever known." He concluded the newspaper article with which we opened this essay, picking up on this theme.

> Do you think I would have been a success with my inventions had I followed the call of the nightlife? Certainly not. And let the young men of this wonderful country take a tip from one who knows— "always follow the straight and narrow path."[17]

---

16. "Edison at Work on Ebbetts Field," *Brooklyn Daily Eagle*, April 1, 1912, p.3.
17. Edison, "Baseball Greatest Game," loc. cit.

THE STORY OF TED'S WALLET[1]

THOMAS EDISON had six children, three by his first wife, Mary, and three more by his second wife, Mina. Of these, Theodore Miller Edison, born at Glenmont, the Edison estate in the Llewellyn Park community in West Orange (now part of the Thomas Edison National Historical Park), on July 10, 1898, was the youngest. His father was fifty-one years old at the time of Ted's birth.

The most famous Theodore of the era was doubtless Theodore Roosevelt, organizer of a volunteer cavalry regiment he named the Rough Riders, who on July 1, 1898, led his famous—and widely publicized—charge up San Juan Hill in Cuba during the Spanish-American War. Among the Rough Riders was another Theodore, twenty-four-year-old Theodore Miller, Mina Edison's brother. Miller was fatally shot during Roosevelt's charge, dying from his wounds on July 8, a mere two days before the Edisons' youngest boy was born.[2] Ted was named in his honor.

Of all of the Edison children, Ted was the one who came closest to following in his father's footsteps. As a youngster with an interest in science, he performed many "experiments" at Glenmont, earning himself the family nickname "the little laboratory assistant." To others, he was simply Ted. He first attended the Haverford School in Pennsylvania, but in the fall of 1909, transferred to Montclair Military Academy,[3] a partial boarding school located much closer to home in Montclair, New Jersey,

1. Portions of this discussion are based on information obtained through personal correspondence with Leonard DeGraaf, Archivist at the Thomas Edison National Historical Park.
2. David Geary, "A Rough Rider from Chautauqua," *The Chautauquan Daily*, August 18, 2016, found online March 15, 2024, at https://chqdaily.com/2016/08/a-rough-rider-from-chautauqua/.
3. For a brief history of the school, which has gone through several transitions and mergers and is known today as Montclair Kimberley Academy, see the narrative found online April 6, 2024, at https://www.mka.org/about/philosophy-history.

before completing his education with a physics degree from Massachusetts Institute of Technology in 1923, thus becoming the only Edison to hold a college degree. He then worked for the Edison Company, rising to a position directing research, until he eventually formed his own enterprise, Calibron Industries, and even created his own laboratory in West Orange. Theodore Edison died in 1992.[4]

For much of his adult life, Ted Edison was an environmental activist with a particular interest in Monhegan Island, Maine. In 1954, he led the way in establishing a corporate entity to preserve the natural beauty. But what is of particular interest in the present context is the timing of Ted's introduction to the island. Beginning in 1908 or perhaps earlier, the Edison family—and Ted—spent their summers on Monhegan Island. It seems likely, then, that while Ted was acquiring his baseball card collection, he was either vacationing with his family on an island off the coast of Maine or, just afterward, adjusting to life in a new school.[5] We cannot say with certainty where Thomas, his father, was during this period, but we do know that he was sharing reminiscences with Thomas C. Martin for a forthcoming authorized biography and, too, that on July 1, 1909, he began commercial manufacturing of a new type of alkaline storage battery.[6] The first activity may well have been undertaken in whole or in part in Maine, but Edison would almost surely have been on hand in New Jersey for the start-up of battery production, to which he had already devoted much effort.

With all of this as context, there are several possible reasons for Ted's beginning his T206 collection. In addition to his advanced age and deafness, Edison was often distracted by his many business considerations. So, Ted may have been collecting *baseball* cards to express a shared interest that might earn his father's attention. Alternatively, as a soon-to-be teenager with an aloof father, Ted may have been collecting *cigarette* cards featuring baseball players as more of a challenge to

4. See the National Park Service's biographical sketch, "Theodore Miller Edison," found online March 15, 2024, at https://www.nps.gov/edis/learn/historyculture/theodore-miller-edison.htm.

5. Theodore M. Edison, "Notes on the Background and Early History of Mohegan Associates, Inc.," found online March 15, 2024, at https://monheganassociates.org/who-we-are/ted-edisons-story/.

6. See the Edison chronology provided by the Edison Papers Project at Rutgers University, found online March 15, 2024, at https://edison.rutgers.edu/life-of-edison/chronology/1901–1910.

his father, juxtaposing Thomas's aversion to cigarette smoking (see the next section) with his love of the game. Third, Ted may have read that first Zane Grey baseball novel, aimed at young boys and published in 1909, and been inspired to begin his collection. Fourth, he might have seen cigarette advertisements mentioning the cards in the newspapers, a common element of such promotions in that period (see an example of this below), or heard about them from a friend and become interested. Fifth, he might have been drawn into the hobby by his new classmates at Montclair and even seen it as a way to fit in. Or, Ted may simply have stumbled across the baseball card hobby fortuitously in some other way, taken an interest, and pursued it for several months or even a year. As we will argue below, once he had begun his collection, it seems likely that Ted was an active trader of cards, which would have been a common social activity in his age cohort and at his new school. Whatever his reason for obtaining them and in whatever ways he enjoyed them, it is worth noting that, after gathering them over a relatively short period, he held onto these cards, which had no special monetary value for much of that time, for the remainder of his life.

We know that Ted Edison carried around his baseball card collection in a wallet that has survived to this day. The wallet, pictured on the following page, was made of leather with a clear window inside and resembled nothing so much as a current-day checkbook cover. It is labeled as a promotional item from the United States Hotel, 26 Cone Street, in Orange, New Jersey.

Though we cannot say with any certainty how Ted might have obtained this wallet, we can date it to 1909 in two ways. First, the design of the wallet includes a faux postage stamp with a postmark of January 1, 1909, which, in apparent celebration of the new year, is consistent with its promotional nature. Second, the wallet identifies "M. Goward" as the proprietor of the hotel. An examination of the relevant city directories for the period shows that in 1908, the proprietor of the hotel was not Goward but Mrs. Marie J. Kazenmayer, while Charles J. Goward was a letter carrier living elsewhere in Orange. But the 1910 directory listed Mr. Goward as the proprietor of the hotel, as did an advertisement in the same book. By 1916, the next available edition of the directory,

Exterior view of Ted's wallet

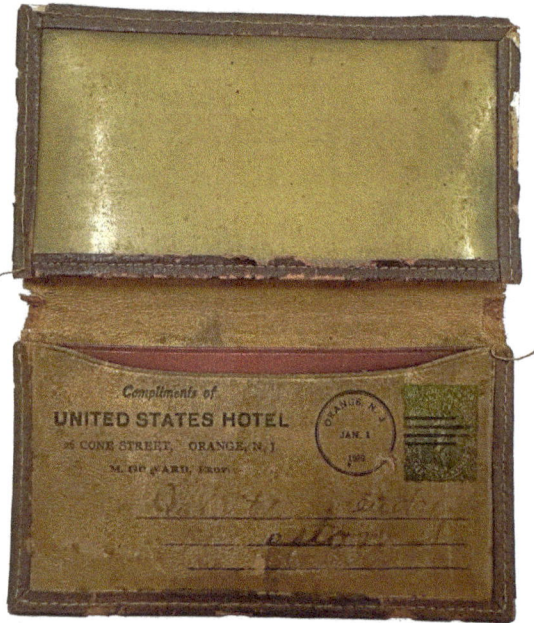

Interior view of Ted's wallet

Mr. Goward, had been replaced by Thomas H. Lipsitt. M. Goward was undoubtedly a relative of Charles J. Goward, leading to the conclusion that that family was, for a brief period corresponding with the date on the wallet, operating the United States Hotel.[7] As we will note below, the dating of the wallet to around 1909 is entirely consistent with the distribution dates for the cards that Ted carried around in it, which adds to the likelihood that the collection was made contemporaneously and in real-time, and not at some later date.

On one side of the interior of the wallet is a clear window that appears to be a plastic of some sort, almost surely a form of celluloid, the only clear plastic that was in general use at the time. Ted's wallet shows cracking, loose threads, torn binding, and other general signs of wear and tear that, even allowing for the passage of more than a century in storage, are all indicative of an item that was carried around and manipulated on a daily basis by an eleven- or twelve-year-old boy. This set of T206 baseball cards was, for some time, however brief it may have been, very much an object of interest for Ted. And then his day-to-day interest seems to have ended. The collection includes very few of the later 350-460 series from 1910 and nothing after that. Again, we cannot be sure. But a simple explanation suggests itself: A *boy* of eleven or twelve might well collect baseball cards to trade with his friends; but a *young man* in his thirteenth year might well be attracted to other, more "mature" pursuits.

One notable question does remain: How did Ted obtain these cards?

As we will discuss in more detail momentarily, the cards were distributed only as promotional items in nickel or dime packages of cigarettes. A reasonable estimate would be that the entire collection, including the cigarettes, would have cost just over three dollars. But we can be fairly certain that Ted, a young boy, was not the purchaser. The wallet itself might offer one clue as to who it was. As noted, the interior is designed to resemble a postcard, complete with a printed-on stamp and postmark. A name and address are, in fact, written in the address block in long-hand—perhaps those of the cigarette smoker in question. Unfortunately,

---

7. Selected directories serving "The Oranges" from this period are available online from the library in Maplewood, New Jersey. See for example http///www.digifind-it.com/IDIViewer/web/viewer.html?file=/maplewood/data/City-Directories/1910/1910_p3.pdf, found online February 25, 2024.

both are largely illegible except that from the remainder, we can be sure the "addressee" was not Ted Edison. Nor is there any evidence to suggest that his father, Thomas, had anything to do with its acquisition.

Whatever their source, it would seem that Ted regarded these cards as personally important—enough so that he held onto them for more than eighty years. When following his death in 1992 at age ninety-four and the passing of his wife, Ann, the following year, the family offered the National Park Service a variety of historical artifacts and documents that had been kept either in their Llewellyn Park home or in Ted's West Orange office, among the personal papers, laboratory records, business records, and seventy-five linear feet of Edison Company records accepted by the Park Service was one well-worn wallet filled with several dozen old baseball cards.

The Irony of Ted's Wallet

ALL T206 CARDS, including all of those in Ted's Wallet, were available only as premiums with the purchase of packs of cigarettes. The Piedmont-backed and Sweet Caporal-backed cards in Ted's collection came in foil-lined packs or ten-count slide and shell boxes that were advertised for sale at five cents apiece, while the Tolstoi-backed cards also came in twenty-count boxes that were flatter and wider than the others and were advertised for a dime.[1] These were three of the fifteen various cigarette and tobacco packs associated with the T206s, all of which shared one thing in common. All of these were brands made by a single manufacturer—the American Tobacco Company. And since Ted collected his cards openly, carrying them around in the aforementioned wallet, even absent evidence either way, it is reasonable to believe that his father, baseball lover Thomas Edison, knew of the collection and at least tacitly approved of his son's hobby. He might even have encouraged it.

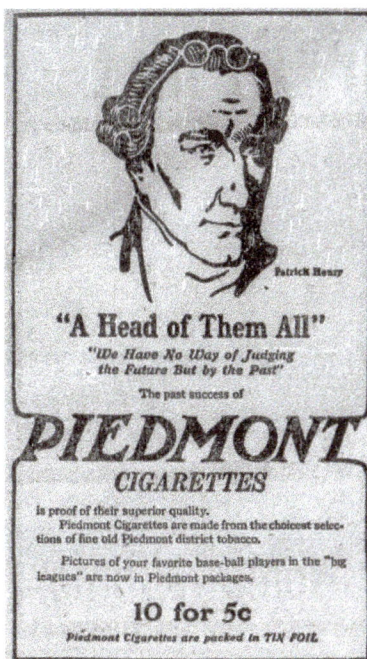

Piedmont Cigarette Ad[2]

1. "1909-1911 T206," found online March 15, 2024, at http://www.baseballandtobacco.com/t206.htm.
2. Piedmont Cigarette advertisements with renderings of such national heroes as Benjamin Franklin, George Washington, or, as in this example, Patrick Henry, appeared in many newspapers around the country. Prominently featured in these ads was the promotion of the baseball cards we now know as the T206s. This advertisement appeared in the March 24, 1910, edition of the *Waco Times-Herald*, p. 9.

Edison was undoubtedly familiar with so-called cigarette cards. He himself had been featured on such a card distributed in 1888 by W. Duke Sons & Company, the manufacturer that later created the American Tobacco Company trust, as part of its Great Americans series, again in 1894 and 1901 in Ogden's "Guinea Gold" Cigarettes New Series 1, and even in France in 1900 in a Félix Potin cigarette card series picturing famous world figures.

It is ironic, then, that just a few years later, in 1914, Edison, with the encouragement and support of his friend Henry Ford, became the public face of a campaign against the smoking of cigarettes and the bête noire of Percival S. Hill, president of the American Tobacco Company. The controversy began when Edison penned this letter to Ford.

Edison to Ford [3]

---

3. Edison letter to Ford dated April 26, 1914, courtesy of Thomas Edison NHP archives, Thomas Edison Papers, Box 236, 1914 Cigarettes.

The letter is notable for several points. First, it identifies the source of the "injurious agent" in cigarettes, not as the tobacco, but as the paper used to wrap it, and the agent itself as acrolein. This distinction is worth noting since Edison himself was a cigar smoker and used chewing tobacco. Second, it states that this acrolein attacks the nerve cells and produces degeneration of the brain. Third, it states that this effect is rapid "among boys," permanent, and uncontrollable. And last, it notes that Edison employs no person who uses cigarettes.

This letter was not written out of the blue. Several weeks earlier, Ford had written to Edison asking him for his views on the subject. This may have occurred over the course of a winter visit by Henry, Clara, and Edsel Ford to the Edisons' winter home in Fort Myers, a visit that fixed the friendship between the two industrialists and led the Fords to build a neighboring winter cottage just two years later. Once he received Edison's response, Ford wasted no time in putting it to use. He determined to have the letter reproduced and framed, then placed in schools around the country, beginning with those in Detroit and Highland Park, Michigan. He announced his campaign the first week in May and assigned his secretary, E.G. Liebold, to fulfill his commitment.[4] Related stories appeared in newspapers around the country, while Ford followed up by publishing a series of three pamphlets under the title *The Case Against the Little White Slaver*.[5]

Whether on purpose or coincidentally, on May 7, 1914, the same day that Ford went public with Edison's letter and began his campaign against cigarettes, the smoking tobacco department of the American Tobacco Company dispatched a letter to Clarence Hayes, an Edison confidante who was serving as manager of the newly formed Edison Baseball Club, offering to equip the team free of charge, including major league-quality uniforms from the Spalding Company, if its members could collect enough labels from sacks of Bull Durham smoking tobacco to win a local contest. The letter went on to suggest that the manager

4. "Henry Ford in Fight Against Cigarette Evil: Won Over By Letter From Thomas A. Edison Telling of Ravages of 'Coffin Nails,'" *Detroit Times*, May 7, 1914, p.3. Note that, the headline notwithstanding, the Edison letter had been requested by Ford and made no reference to coffin nails.

5. Found online March 12, 2024, at https://www.thehenryford.org/collections-and-research/digital-collections/artifact/374491.

might facilitate the effort by encouraging patrons to attend games by paying their admission with ten Bull Durham labels rather than cash.[6] It is worth noting that Bull Durham tobacco was advertised on the basis of price (enough tobacco to roll forty cigarettes for a nickel, compared with the ten manufactured cigarettes the same amount would purchase) and an appeal to ego—"Experienced Smokers 'Roll Their Own'"—including an offer to provide free cigarette papers with each sack purchased.[7]

Not surprisingly, Ford's initiative occasioned a backlash from the industry. On May 18, shortly after the news coverage reached a crescendo, Edison received a five-page letter from Mr. Hill, who opened by asserting that.

> These statements are so erroneous and so misleading that in justice to the millions of intelligent men who use cigarettes we are compelled to resent your unjustified attack . . . Since your prominence and fame give your words greater weight than the words of men of no importance there is imposed upon you a corresponding responsibility to make no statement reflecting on a product—and on millions of users of such product—without investigation and the certainty that comes from investigation.[8]

In short—and the letter was anything but short—Hill challenged Edison to prove the validity of his assertions. He went on to cite a number of studies proving the safety of cigarette use, and to accuse the inventor of imposing his personal preferences on his employees by denying them the pleasure of smoking cigarettes.

Hill's letter seems to have struck a nerve because Edison responded the very next day saying that the news accounts were mistaken in that he had never prohibited, nor asked the six thousand employees in his factories to refrain from, smoking cigarettes. Then he added, "However, in my Laboratory, I have for a long time had a sign up forbidding my

---

6. Correspondence from the Smoking Tobacco Department to Hayes dated May 7, 1914, found in the archives of the Thomas Edison National Historical Park.

7. See for example an advertisement in the *Washington Post*, June 14, 1914, p. 50.

8. Letter from Hill to Edison dated May 18, 1914, found online at https://edisondigital.rutgers.edu/document/E1423AE#. Provided by the Thomas A. Edison Papers at Rutgers University.

experimenters from using tobacco in this form—I have abundant reasons for thinking they are much worse than tobacco in other forms." Edison closed with an offer to "put a couple of my men on the experiment & get facts." The first draft of this letter is shown here.

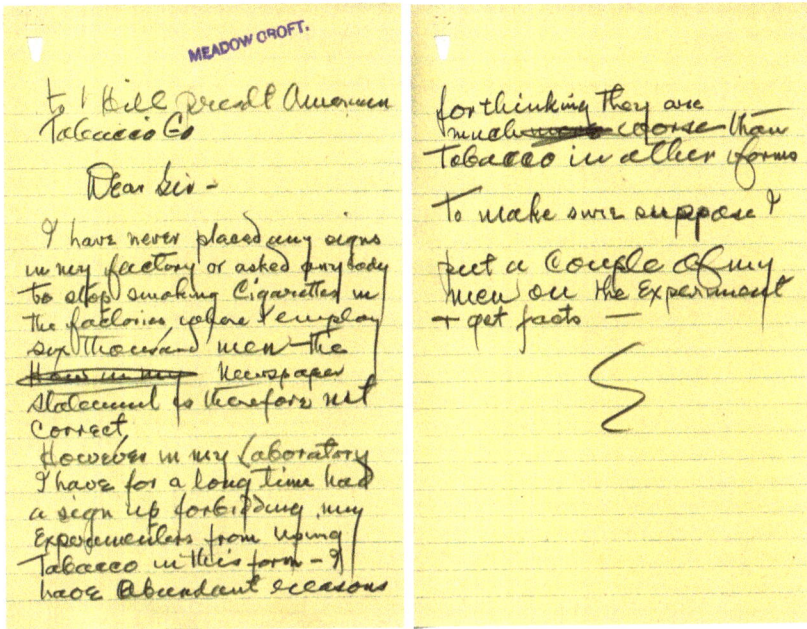

Draft Letter to Percival Hill [9]

In the meantime, on May 17, the *Brooklyn Eagle* newspaper had opined that Edison's claims of knowing the medical effects of acrolein, the supposed injurious agent produced by burning cigarette papers, was knowledge he held at best only second hand. [10] This was an insult Edison could not endure, and on May 20, he penned a letter to the editor of the newspaper in which he noted:

At one time I almost lost my life through the breaking of a glass tube filled with acrolein. On another occasion one of my assistants was

9. Edison's draft letter to Hill dated, finalized and dispatched on May 19, 1914, courtesy of Thomas Edison NHP archives, Thomas Edison Papers, Box 236, 1914 Cigarettes.
10. "Ford-Edison War on Cigarettes," *Brooklyn Eagle*, May 17, 1914, p.16, found online March 12, 2024, at https://www.newspapers.com/image/685821150/.

almost killed in an experiment where that substance was produced unexpectedly. For more than two years I experimented continuously on the burning, carbonizing and distilling of all kinds of paper in the attempt to make suitable filaments therefrom for incandescent lamps. I believe I can justly claim that some of my information is not second hand.[11]

The correspondence with American Tobacco continued on May 22, when Mr. Hill wrote to Edison accepting his offer to investigate the effects of acrolein but also noting that he had consulted with a local doctor who had told him that acrolein was produced whenever any kind of fat is burned, that cigarette paper like all papers contained an "infinitely small" amount of fat, and that consuming cigarettes at the rate of twenty per day it would take a smoker three years to produce even a gram of acrolein, which would, in any event, have been eliminated from his system over those same three years.[12] Edison replied by repeating the points he had made to the Brooklyn newspaper editor and reiterated his offer to have the matter investigated.[13]

While this latter correspondence appears to have assuaged Mr. Hill, his was not the only rebuttal to Edison's attack on cigarettes. On June 24, the half-page advertisement on the following page appeared in *The New York Times* and was then placed in many newspapers around the country in the days that followed.

Note the subhead: "The greater the man, the greater his ventures, the greater his achievements, and the greater his MISTAKES." It would have been impossible for anyone, let alone Edison, to have missed the highly personal nature of this attack. This was too much even for Percival Hill, who wrote the letter on page 22 to Edison that same day.

---

11. Edison letter to Editor, Brooklyn Eagle, dated May 20, 1914, found online March 12, 2024, at https://edisondigital.rutgers.edu/document/E1423AJ#. Provided by the Thomas A. Edison Papers at Rutgers University.

12. Hill letter to Edison dated May 22, 1914, found online March 12, 2024, at https://edisondigital.rutgers.edu/document/E1423AK#. Provided by the Thomas A. Edison Papers at Rutgers University.

13. May 19, 1914, handwritten letter (possibly a draft) from Edison to Hill found online March 12, 2024, at https://edisondigital.rutgers.edu/document/E1423AH#. Provided by the Thomas A. Edison Papers at Rutgers University.

IT WAS
MR. EDISON'S
MISTAKE

The greater the man the greater his ventures, the greater his achievements, and the greater his MISTAKES.

¶ MR. THOS. A. EDISON, the great inventor and scientist, has recently made a great mistake.
¶ He made a statement to the effect that the cigarette is injurious, on the alleged ground that he has found poisonous matter in the PAPER wrapper of some twenty different brands which he has analyzed.
¶ This statement was printed in the newspapers a few weeks ago. In the meantime, several protests have appeared in certain newspapers and trade papers, disproving the presence of any poison in the cigarette paper and making it clear that the substance which Mr. Edison has found, and which he calls "poison," is NOT poison.
¶ These protests were incontestible. They were based upon the results of scientific investigations and careful analyses previously made by unquestionably the most reliable chemical authorities, including the London "Lancet," the foremost medical organization in the world.
¶ Mr. Edison's contention involved all the cigarettes in general, no mention being made of any particular brand or brands; and so did the answers resenting Mr. Edison's unjustified attack.
¶ However, I do not think that the general character of the matter exempts the individual cigarette manufacturer from the duty to prove in a specific, definite and indubitable manner the purity of the particular brand of paper in which HIS particular brand of cigarettes are wrapped. I think each manufacture owes this procedure to himself and to the public, in order to remove such unfavorable impression of his goods as Mr. Edison's erroneous and misleading statement may have left in the minds of those among his the manufacture's present and prospective patrons, who may, in their turn, make the mistake of granting that just because Mr. Edison is a genius in ELECTRICITY, he is also infallible in his findings in ANALYTICAL CHEMISTRY.
¶ We all appreciate the fact that Mr. Edison has acquired and he maintains his prominence and fame in the most honest and deserving way, and we feel indebted to him for the most useful service he has rendered to humanity, as a wonderfully able electrician and mechanic.
¶ BUT WHEN IT COMES TO ANALYTICAL CHEMISTRY, I BELIEVE MR. EDISON HIMSELF WILL ADMIT THAT SUPREMACY IN THAT BRANCH OF SCIENCE BELONGS TO OTHERS.
¶ When I read Mr. Edison's statement in the newspapers I was particularly interested in it because I have, among my accounts, the advertising of the well-known

Philip Morris Cigarettes,

and it is part of my business to further the interests of PHILIP MORRIS & CO., LTD., by a correct representation of their goods to the public.
¶ I immediately decided to resent publicly Mr. Edison's attack. I was as positive at that time as I am now that the paper in which PHILIP MORRIS CIGARETTES are wrapped is absolutely the best and the purest paper made and free from any poisonous ingredients. But I did not want to base my protest upon mere personal knowledge or opinion, nor did I deem it sufficient to refer to any reports or certificates previously issued in favor of cigarettes IN GENERAL.
¶ My share of the task, as stated above, being to defend the PHILIP MORRIS CIGARETTES in PARTICULAR, it was necessary for me to present to the public the results of a SPECIAL investigation and a chemical analysis proving the purity of the PARTICULAR brand of paper in which PHILIP MORRIS CIGARETTES are wrapped.
¶ I could not very well hurry with the work. It required time to gather the necessary information from both the manufacturers of the PHILIP MORRIS CIGARETTES and the manufacturer of the PAPER used for wrapping the PHILIP MORRIS CIGARETTES, and subject this paper to a chemical analysis.
¶ This analysis alone took about two weeks. It was made in the most complete and careful manner by Ricketts & Banks of New York, who rank among the most reliable analytical chemists in the country and who have issued a certificate to the effect that NO POISONOUS INGREDIENTS COULD BE FOUND IN THE PAPER IN WHICH PHILIP MORRIS CIGARETTES ARE WRAPPED.
¶ The following is a fac-simile of the text of the said certificate, the original of which is in my possession, and can be seen by any one, upon request.

Analysis No. 27762

James Zobian Company,
225 Fifth Ave.,
New York City.

Gentlemen:

Referring to the sample of paper marked "Philip Morris Cigarette" submitted to us for analysis we have to report that we are unable to find any poisonous ingredients therein.

Yours very truly,

Ricketts & Banks

¶ I always keep myself informed with the sales of my clients.
1. MR. EDISON'S STATEMENT APPEARED IN THE NEWSPAPERS ON MAY 11TH.
2. ON MONDAY, MAY 18TH, MORE PHILIP MORRIS CIGARETTES WERE SOLD THAN ON ANY OTHER DAY IN THE LAST SIXTY YEARS.
3. THE BUSINESS ON PHILIP MORRIS CIGARETTES FOR THE MONTH OF MAY WAS LARGER THAN THAT OF ANY OTHER MONTH IN THE LAST SIXTY YEARS, WITH A CONSIDERABLE INCREASE OVER THE PREVIOUS BEST MONTH.
4. THE MONTH OF JUNE WILL BE EVEN MORE PROSPEROUS THAN MAY, PROVIDING THE SALES CONTINUE AT THE SAME RATE DURING THE REMAINDER OF THE MONTH AS IN THE FIRST THREE WEEKS.
¶ This increase in the sales of PHILIP MORRIS CIGARETTES, following Mr. Edison's attack, may have been a coincidence, but it may also be due to the public tendency to take special precautions, in such circumstances, by giving preference to the product which is the BEST KNOWN, the LONGEST KNOWN and the MOST WIDELY KNOWN in its field.
¶ The public knows that the longer a product enjoys FAVORABLE PUBLIC OPINION and confidence the more evident is its quality.
¶ The public also knows today that the PHILIP MORRIS CIGARETTE is THE CIGARETTE which has enjoyed the most favorable opinion and continuous patronage of the most critical smokers throughout the world, for unquestionably THE LONGEST period of time in the history of high-grade Turkish Cigarettes.
¶ Although Mr. Edison's unjustified attack involved only the paper and not the tobacco—of cigarettes, I believe, however, that the following extract from a report issued by the London "Lancet," the greatest chemical authority in the world, will also be of particular interest to Mr. Edison as a cigar smoker, pipe lover, tobacco chewer and cigarette hater:

It was found that the CIGARETTE, whether Egyptian, Turkish, or American, yielded the LEAST AMOUNT of its total nicotine to the smoke formed, THE PIPE YIELDED A VERY LARGE PROPORTION (in some cases 70 to 80 per cent.) of its nicotine to the smoke reaching the mouth of the consumer; and the analysis of cigar smoke gave figures midway between the two. From the point of view of nicotine poisoning, therefore, assuming that equal amounts of tobacco were smoked THE CIGARETTE WOULD APPEAR TO BE THE LEAST HARMFUL FORM OF SMOKING, and the pipe the worst; the cigar occupying an intermediate position in this respect, judging from the amount of nicotine contained in the smoke therefrom.

JAMES ZOBIAN, Advertising Agent,
225 Fifth Avenue, New York.

Philip Morris Ad[14]

14. This advertisement appeared first in *The New York Times*, June 24, 1914, p.3.

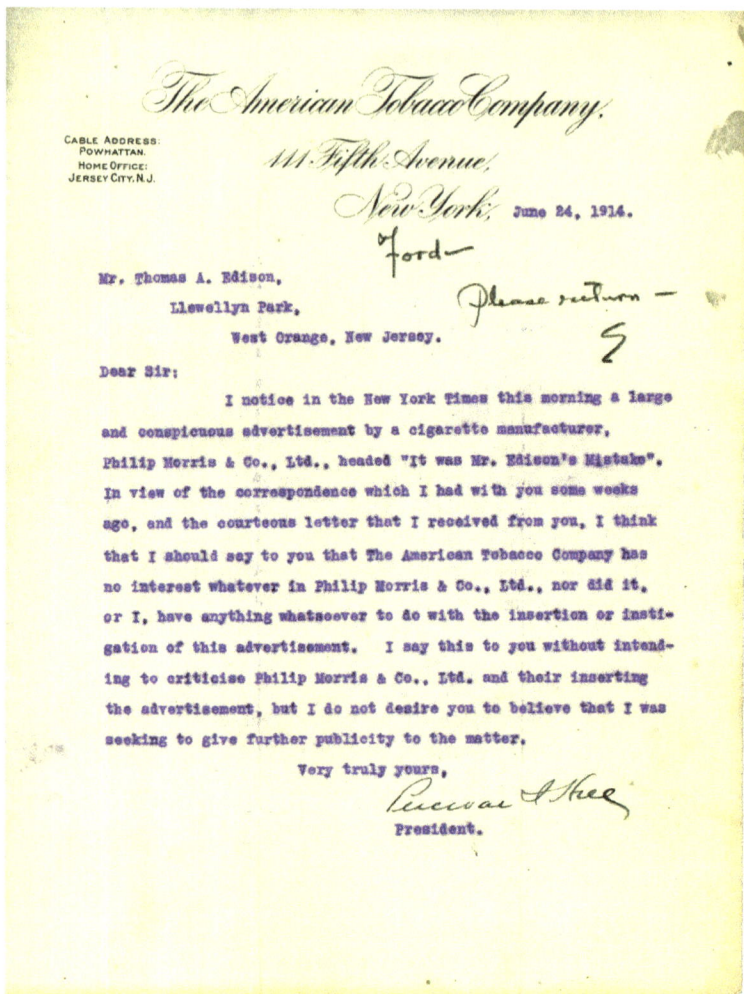

Hill letter to Edison[15]

In this letter, Hill was obviously trying to de-escalate his dispute with Edison, even as he tried to maintain industry solidarity with a rival manufacturer, Philip Morris. Per the notation at the top, Edison forwarded this letter to Ford, who responded through his secretary, Mr. Liebold, on July 1 that he had brought this matter to the attention of the *Detroit Times*, which had, in turn, published a lengthy and detailed

---

15. Letter from Hill to Edison dated June 24, 1914, courtesy of Thomas Edison NHP archives, Thomas Edison Papers, Box 236, 1914 Cigarettes.

defense (which he attached) pointing out that Edison was being accused of making claims against cigarettes that he (and Ford) had never made. Further, Liebold indicated that he had recruited a magazine writer to produce an additional rebuttal.[16] For his part, Edison was disinclined to engage further through the media. Having received a telegram from a reporter named Agnew at the *Wall Street Journal* requesting a statement or an interview to rebut the charges leveled in the Philip Morris advertising campaign, Edison responded that he "does not care to answer such low type false advertising," then cleverly added that even the American Tobacco Company wanted to disassociate itself from the advertisement. Edison's telegram replying to the newspaper was sent collect.[17]

In the meantime, Edison received several letters from other industry and business notables, most supporting his views on cigarette smoking. He did, however, receive one rather nuanced missive from another tobacco manufacturer, Alexander Haddad, maker of the Egyptian Pharaohs brand of cigarettes which featured potent Turkish tobacco, who praised Edison's initial letter to Ford, then went on to note, "If the cigarettes arrest and dulls [sic] the brains of individuals, it is better so, than have an active mischievous brain, for the man of strong thinking mind smoking will help him deliberate better." He went on to challenge Edison, once having identified the poisonous agent in cigarette paper, to invent an improved paper for this use.[18]

Finally, the archives include Edison's handwritten draft of a June 9, 1914, response to a Mr. J. Cornelius Earll, who had apparently pointed out, as we did above, that Edison himself used tobacco products, in which he notes that:

16. Letter from Liebold, Ford's personal secretary, to W.H. Meadowcroft, Edison's personal secretary, dated July 1, 1914, found online March 12, 2024, at https://edisondigital.rutgers.edu/document/E1423AR#. Provided by the Thomas A. Edison Papers at Rutgers University; and "Issue Dodged By the Friends of Cigarettes: Answer 'Charges' That Henry Ford and T.A. Edison Have Never Made," *Detroit Times*, June 29, 1914, pp.1, 9.

17. Agnew telegram to Meadowcroft dated June 27, 1914, found online March 12, 2024, at https://edisondigital.rutgers.edu/document/E1423AP#; and text of Meadowcroft response to Agnew as directed by Edison dated June 27, 1914, found online March 12, 2024, at https://edisondigital.rutgers.edu/document/E1423AQ#. Provided by the Thomas A. Edison Papers at Rutgers University.

18. Letter from Haddad to Edison dated May 11, 1914, found online March 12, 2024, at https://edisondigital.rutgers.edu/document/E1423AC#?. Provided by the Thomas A. Edison Papers at Rutgers University.

I cannot defend my using tobacco for chewing—it is a habit I got when a young telegraph operator whose smoking was not allowed. It appears that the cells of the body will meet the [ILLEGIBLE] of the body and adapt the body to such [ILLEGIBLE] and after so adapting, the cells resent any change.[19]

In other words, Edison acknowledged that he was addicted to chewing tobacco. And we know from many sources, not least the story about the visit of the Philadelphia baseball team, that he was a regular smoker of strong cigars. None of this kept him from—or perhaps it motivated him in—leading an assault on the use of cigarettes, particularly on the part of young boys. Moreover, he made clear in these various exchanges that his view of the hazards of cigarette smoking had been long-standing.

And indeed it had. In an interview quoted in the *Carbondale Leader* of June 14, 1906, fully three years before his son Ted began collecting baseball cards, Edison said

Smoking tobacco is a pretty good working stimulant. But cigarettes, they're deadly. It isn't the tobacco, it's the acrolein produced by burning the paper that does the harm, and let me tell you—his voice betrayed some feeling and his face grew graver—acrolein is one of the most terrible drugs in its effect on the human body. . . . I really believe it often makes boys insane. . . . I can hardly exaggerate the dangerous nature of acrolein, and yet that is what a man or a boy is dealing with every time he smokes an ordinary cigarette. The harm that such a deadly poison when taken into the system must inflict upon a growing boy is horrible to contemplate.[20]

Even at that early date, Edison's view was widely known, and was even cited in the British press.[21]

His view of cigarettes was prominently featured again in August, 1911, when, on a family visit to Switzerland that included son Ted, the

---

19. Draft letter to Earll dated June 9, 1914, found online March 12, 2024, at https://edisondigital. rutgers.edu/document/E1423AM1#. Provided by the Thomas A. Edison Papers at Rutgers University.

20. "Cigarette Smoking," the *Carbondale Leader*, June 14, 1906, p. 4.

21. "Joseph Hatton, "Cigarette Papers: For After-Dinner Smoking," a column that appeared, for example, in the *Staffordshire Sentinel* (Stoke-on-Trent, England), October 13, 1906, p. 2.

Edisons were nearly killed when the car in which they were riding slid off a mountain road and came close to dropping fifty feet to a river below. It took a farmer with a team of oxen to pull the vehicle to safety. The Edisons were accompanied on their tour by a correspondent for the *St. Louis Post-Dispatch* and the *New York World*, and in a wide-ranging interview about his experiences and his views on the countries he had visited the inventor observed

> I did notice that every Frenchman had a cigarette in his mouth. It is the cigarette that causes their degeneracy. It is not the tobacco, it is the paper wrapping. The curse of absinthe is nothing compared to that of cigarettes.[22]

It is little surprise then, that Edison's ideas about tobacco use would make their way to the baseball diamond. In February 1914, even as Edison and Ford were vacationing together in Florida, Branch Rickey, newly appointed as manager of the St. Louis Browns in the American League and destined to become one of the most innovative executives in the game, adopted a distinctly Edison-style position with respect to his players. As the team arrived in St. Peterburg, Florida, just up the coast from the inventor's winter compound, Rickey announced that his players would not be permitted to use cigarettes because of their "poisoned paper." "I think the use of cigarettes is injurious to the players," he said. In their stead, Rickey noted, he had purchased an ample supply of cigars which he would freely provide to any player seeking a smoke.[23]

One can only wonder, then, what the inventor's feelings were as he tolerated, or perhaps encouraged, his young son Theodore to collect baseball cards that could only be obtained by supporting the smoking of cigarettes—doing the math, more than six hundred of them over a few months—and, too, who close to the family might have been risking Edison's wrath by engaging in that habit and acquiring the cards for Ted.

---

22. "Thomas A. Edison Says: America Is Mentally, Morally and Physically Supreme . . . ," *St. Louis Post-Dispatch*, September 3, 1911, p. 14; and "Edison and His Family Nearly Thrown Into an Abyss by Skidding Auto," *St. Louis Post-Dispatch*, August 29, 1911, p. 12.

23. "Rickey Keeps His Players in Cigars," *Dayton Herald*, February 27, 1914, p. 21.

The Deadball Era in Baseball: A Special Time, A Special Game

BASEBALL EMERGED from a number of ball-and-bat games during the middle years of the nineteenth century and evolved from a pick-up game to a club sport. The game was widely played by soldiers during the Civil War, and afterward many players and observers began to take it more seriously, enough so that the better players came to be paid for their efforts. The National League, the first self-declared "major" baseball league, was formed in 1876. Over the next quarter century, other leagues aspired to equivalent status, sometimes raiding the National League team rosters to raise and legitimize their quality of play. None of these challenges succeeded until two men, Ban Johnson and Charles Comiskey, took over a minor circuit called the Western League, recast it as the American League, and began, like their predecessors, to raid and otherwise challenge the National League franchises. This time, the insurgency was successful enough that the National League was forced to sue for peace. In 1903 the two circuits signed a treaty, called the National Agreement, that was meant to impose a unifying structure on professional baseball from the major leagues on down, and created a National Commission to govern the sport. What followed was a remarkable period of on-field play and off-field development that, in many ways, define our perceptions of the game to this day.

Baseball historians refer to the first decades of this professionalization, roughly between 1900 and 1920, as the Deadball Era. The term is a retrofit to the period, as we will see momentarily. In addition to the two so-called "major" leagues, the nation was endowed with a plethora of lesser, so-called "minor" leagues that, because of the cost and inconvenience of long-distance travel, were defined on relatively localized geographic bases—state, multi-state, or regional. With the exception of certain leagues that, from time to time, claimed to be independent of such structure, these were assigned grades ranging from AA to F that were meant to characterize their respective qualities of play. These grades, however, were hardly fixed, and the same league might attain a given level, or "class," in one year and a different one the next. Nor was their membership fixed and certain. Teams representing various cities within the geographic footprint of each league entered or departed and routinely changed their monikers from one season to the next. The names of these teams reflected anything from the nature of the local workforce to the color of their uniforms to the prejudices of the local population.

The Deadball Era was the epoch of many of baseball's best-remembered players—Christy Mathewson and Ty Cobb, Honus Wagner and Walter Johnson, Home Run Baker and Frank Chance, to name but a few. But as importantly or more so, it was a time when baseball came of age. The National Agreement and the National Commission gave the game structure, but it needed something more. It needed mythos. And in 1907, former player and then sporting goods mogul Albert Spalding, who had helped to found the National League, provided that through the report of a commission of his own, called the Mills Commission, that declared baseball to be an inherently American game invented in an inherently American place, Cooperstown, New York, by a true American military hero, Abner Doubleday. Today, that declaration is largely discounted, but at the time, it was taken as gospel, providing the necessary underpinning to the claim of baseball to be the National Pastime. The Deadball Era also saw the beginning of the World Series, the dismantling of yet another would-be major league, the Federal League, which soon led to a court decision that effectively exempted baseball from the newly enacted antitrust laws, rules changes, equipment changes, and more. Not all of these developments were positive, of course, and the era ended badly with the so-called Black Sox gambling scandal in the 1919 World Series. In its wake, in 1920, baseball reorganized itself once again, creating the all-powerful Office of the Commissioner of Baseball and hiring its first occupant, Judge Kenesaw Mountain Landis.

In all of this, baseball was a creature of its times. With its 1898 victory in the Spanish-American War, the United States found itself a nascent colonial empire with interests stretching from Cuba to the Philippines and the Hawaiian Islands. Shortly afterward, the self-created hero of that conflict, Theodore Roosevelt, whom we met earlier, ushered in the modern American presidency with his contagious energy, progressive ideas, and thirst for publicity. The economy began to shift more rapidly from an agrarian base to an industrial one, and the huge sector-specific trusts that had been formed by such men as Carnegie, Rockefeller, and Gould came under pressure from new laws designed to break them up. And there was more. Powered flight. Mass production. Mass audience media. Expanded public education. Imposition of the income tax. World War I. Prohibition. Women's suffrage. The first pandemic of the modern era. It was in this social and political hothouse environment that baseball prospered, gained in popularity, and became a central element of American daily life.

Put another way, baseball grew into itself. It matured in ways that maintained its fit within the larger cultural milieu. Like the society itself in 1900, baseball was a somewhat pastoral activity. The games did not take long to play—about two hours for nine innings—but they were, by today's standards, leisurely affairs. Baseballs not only stayed in the park most of the time, but they stayed in the game. The same ball might be used for the entire game, even as it became discolored with tobacco juice and dirt or disfigured with repeated strikes of a bat. It was only when the ball became disassembled—literally coming apart at the seams—that an umpire might replace it. And as one might expect, as the game wore on, these less visible, less resilient, and less structurally sound balls traveled less far with less velocity. Finesse could be more important than power in determining the outcome.

But as society changed—sped up, if you will—so, of necessity and the natural order of things, did baseball. The core of the baseball was redesigned, and the stitching was standardized. Umpires were instructed to replace the balls more often during a game. And beginning in 1920, the official baseballs were stitched by machines rather than by hand, making them more consistent from one to the next. In 1909, when

Ted Edison began collecting his baseball cards, Ty Cobb led the major leagues in home runs with nine. In 1920, Babe Ruth led the major leagues in home runs with fifty-four. The headstone of the Deadball Era had been set.

It was precisely in the middle of this period, from 1909 to 1911, that American Tobacco published the T206 series of baseball cards. There were five hundred fourteen cards in the series (including a number of variations for some players), and together, they not only pictured many players of the era from the major and minor leagues alike, but somehow, to our modern sensibilities, they captured as well the romanticism of baseball in its early days. Some of the players' names still resonate today, but for a true baseball fan, the romance and simplicity associated with them are, at some deep level, the true cornerstone of the game. It is that, and not simply the age or imputed economic value of some often imperfect souvenirs from cigarette boxes, that helps to explain the allure of these ancient bits of cardboard.

Ted, of course, would neither have known nor appreciated any of that in his twelfth year. For him, surely, collecting these images of the icons of a game that his father loved and that he likely did as well would have afforded a full measure of enjoyment in itself.

The T206 Baseball Cards: Capturing Baseball's Glory Days

In 1890, J.B. Duke created the American Tobacco Company through the merger of what eventually numbered more than two hundred manufacturers. It was one of the original twelve companies included in the Dow Jones Industrial Average in 1896. American Tobacco quickly came to dominate the industry, but only for a short time. As part of the trust-busting activism of the era, the federal government succeeded in breaking the company up into several major competitors.[1] That effort culminated in 1911, which, probably not by coincidence, was also the final year of the T206 card promotion.

The white border cards issued by the American Tobacco Company from 1909 through 1911, depicting baseball players from the major and minor leagues, were assigned the designation of T206—the "T" meaning tobacco cards—by Jefferson Burdick in his 1939 book, *The United States Card Collectors Catalog* and have been identified by that label ever since. These cards were inserted in cigarette packs or other tobacco products as promotional premiums. They were produced in three series: the 150, 350, and 460. The series denotes the approximate number of players included in each. Upon issue in 1909, only 150 players were included. The set then expanded to 350 later in 1909, meaning 200 players were added to the set. By mid-1910, another 110 players were added, expanding the set to 460 players.[2]

---

1. James L. Hunt, "United States v. American Tobacco Company," *Encyclopedia of North Carolina*, 2006, found online April 7, 2024, at https://www.ncpedia.org/united-states-v-american-tobacco-co.

2. Lew Lipset, *The Encyclopedia of Baseball Cards: Volumes 1,2 & 3 Combined* (The Vintage and Classic Baseball Card Magazine, Tacoma, WA, 1987), pp. 46-47.

Serious collectors of T206 cards are familiar with the variety of backs that could occur. Each back represented a particular tobacco product. Following is a list of the backs known to exist with T206 cards and their relative scarcity:

T206 Backs/Population/Series[3]				
Brand	% Pop	150	350	460
Piedmont	51	x	x	x
Sweet Caporal	26	x	x	x
Old Mill	5			x
Polar Bear	4.25	x	x	x
Sovereign	4.25	x	x	x
El Principe de Gales	1.25	x	x	x
Tolstoi	1.25		x	x
American Beauty	1		x	x
Cycle	1		x	x
Hindu	1	x	x	
Carolina Brights	1		x	
Broad Leaf	0.75		x	x
Lenox	0.75			x
Drum	0.75		x	
Uzit	0.75			x
Ty Cobb	0		?	

The Ty Cobb back was only found on a small number of Ty Cobb portrait cards.[4] The red-background portrait of Cobb was also issued in the 350 series with a variety of backs, so the Ty Cobb back was likely issued around the time of the 350.

More recent baseball cards contain statistics or anecdotes about the player or players pictured on them. This is very different from these early

3. Compiled from data from "Reverse Engineering T206 Baseball Card Backs" found online April 6, 2024 at https://www.pwccmarketplace.com/definitive-guides/reverse-engineering-a-guide-to-t206-baseball-card-backs; and Lew Lipset, *The Encyclopedia of Baseball Cards: Volumes 1,2 & 3 Combined* (The Vintage and Classic Baseball Card Magazine, Tacoma, WA, 1987), pp. 47-52.

4. Tom Zapella and Ellen Zapella, *The T206 Collection: The Players and Their Stories, 2nd Edition* (Peter E. Randall, Portsmouth, NH, 2018), p. 208.

cards, which were promoting tobacco products. The only player informa-tion provided is on the front, and that is minimal, for example: "Cobb, Detroit" for the Tiger great.

Serious collectors also focus on the American Tobacco Company factory number located on the back of most of the cards.[5] Following are those recorded:

  6 – Ohio
 17 – Virginia
 25 – Virginia
 30 – New York
 42 – North Carolina
649 – New York

The factory locations would indicate only a small region of the coun-try was involved with the issuance of the cards. Essentially, the territory was New York City to North Carolina and only as far west as Ohio. In those days, the major leagues extended no farther west than St. Louis, Missouri, and no farther south than Washington, DC, in the east. Amer-ican Tobacco's reach was close to all the major league teams. However, the Virginia and North Carolina factories opened the door to include many minor league players, especially those from the Southern League.

Within the series, there were also different printings to capture any changes in portraits or teams. For instance, should a player be traded, his card would likely be updated later in printing. Some of these variations are very scarce, coupled with the particular backs associated with them.

Anytime there is a significant discovery of T206 baseball cards, it catches the attention of the media. In 2016, there was the "Lucky Seven Find" of seven red Ty Cobb cards with very rare Ty Cobb backs found in a paper bag in an old house.[6] The family was cleaning out and was about to throw the bag away before deciding to check the contents. Those lucky descendants happened into a seven-figure find when all was said and done. This story made the national news. Of course, anytime a Honus

5. Lew Lipset, op. cit., p. 53.
6. Zapella and Zapella, op. cit., pp. 206-213.

Wagner card is sold, it also garners attention. An example sold at auction in 2022 for over seven million dollars.[7] Even the common cards are in demand. Near complete sets, less the rarities, can be found for sale for over one hundred thousand dollars.[8]

---

7. Rich Mueller, "$7.25 Million: New Record for T206 Honus Wagner Card," *Sports Collectors Daily*, August 4, 2022, found online April 6, 2024, at https://www.sportscollectorsdaily.com/t206-honus-wagner-sgc-2-sold-record.

8. "1909-11 T206 White Borders" at Dean's Cards, found online April 6, 2024, at https://www.deanscards.com/c/3321/1909-11-T206-Piedmont-Sweet-Caporal-Back.

WHAT'S IN TED'S WALLET?

SO, WHAT TO MAKE of 61 cards found in an old wallet associated with the son of Thomas Alva Edison, the famous inventor?

The vast majority of Ted's cards are from the 350 series with Sweet Caporal backs. They were printed at "Factory 30," which was the New York City facility for the American Tobacco Company. In fact, all the cards but one were from Factory 30. The outlier was a Piedmont card depicting Otto Knabe from the 350 series printed at Factory 25, Richmond, Virginia. Given that only three of the cards were from the 460 series and the rest from the 350, it appears the period they were collected fell between the middle of 1909 and late 1910. Another oddity about Ted's collection is that five of the cards had Tolstoi backs. Did Ted trade for these? Or did his "connection" experiment with other brands, maybe when the Sweet Caporals were out of stock at the local store?

The figure on the following page shows the four distinctive backs, or reverse sides, of the cards in Ted's collection. Note the indications of brand, series, and factory number.

Of course, these days, condition is everything when it comes to card value. Collectors of modern cards expect perfection and have them certified and encased in plastic. Some years ago, collectors would pop cards into albums with polyurethane pages. But going back decades, young collectors would throw them in an old shoebox and tuck them under the bed or in a closet. Those bubblegum cards from the 1950s and 1960s were much larger than the earlier tobacco cards and were sold with a stick of gum added to the pack. The cards were the feature—the gum was the premium.

Selected Reverse Sides of Cards in Ted's Wallet

So, how were T206 cards collected? There are stories of baby boomers in their youth sticking a Mickey Mantle in their bicycle spokes to make a rumbling noise.[1] Fortunately, the T206s were too small for such use! Instead, Ted Edison decided to carry them around with him in his wallet.

---

1. "Mickey Mantle, Jackie Robinson, and More Saved From Bicycle Spokes in The Noise Maker Collection" from Just Collect, found online April 6, 2024, at https://blog.justcollect.com/mickey-mantle-jackie-robinson-and-more-saved-from-bicycle-spokes-in-the-noise-maker-collection.

As you can imagine, anything carried in a wallet will ultimately warp and bend. And, as cards are taken out and put back, there are ample opportunities for further wear and tear. A remarkable aspect of Ted's collection is the evidence of use. Did he pull out his favorites for conversation? Or, was there a game played with classmates—like a card toss or dice game? We can never know. Perusing the collection from a condition perspective will find about a dozen cards with significant creases, bends, or tears. There are two Christy Mathewson cards. One is in rough shape, but the other rough cards are not the most famous players. The worst-conditioned card is the Otto Knabe with the Piedmont back produced in Richmond. It is an outlier in this collection given the brand on the back, the factory number, and the condition. Certainly, there is a story to this card that is very different from the rest!

From a grading perspective, the cards in Ted's collection would likely not do well if sent to a grading service like the Professional Sports Authenticator (PSA), which has become very popular. PSA uses a ten-point scale, with one (Poor) being the worst, up to ten (Mint) being the best.[2] The worst of Ted's cards are less than Pr-1 (Poor) due to excessive wear. Most are Gd-2 (Good), with a few VG-3 (Very Good). All have rounded corners, and quite a few have creases or other imperfections. This is not a group of pristine cards found in old cigarette packs or an old bag under the floorboards. These cards were handled many times. So, given the common backs and mostly common cards in rough condition, this accumulation would not be as remarkable if not for the celebrity connection. Thus, an estimation of value by examining each card would not capture the historical significance of the extant accumulation and its collector.

So, why did Ted focus on these 58 different players, keeping three duplicates (61 cards in total)? There are a good number of Hall of Famers in the group. Of course, the Baseball Hall of Fame in Cooperstown did not open until 1939, long after Ted's wallet was likely forgotten in a drawer or closet. But Ted must have known about Chief Bender,

---

2. "Grading Standards" from Professional Sports Authenticator (PSA), found online April 6, 2024, at https://www.psacard.com/gradingstandards.

Mordecai "Three-Finger" Brown, Frank Chance, Ty Cobb, Hughie Jennings, Walter Johnson, Joe Kelley, Christy Mathewson, and Ted Willis.

Besides the duplicates of Christy Mathewson, Ted also had two examples of Cy Seymour and Paddy Livingston. Mathewson and Seymour both played for the New York Giants. But Livingston played for Connie Mack's Philadelphia Athletics.

From a team perspective, there is evidence Ted may have traded for some cards. Perhaps the New York Giants of the National League were his favorites. He had ten cards from eight different players. He was also heavy on the Eastern League Buffalo Bisons with six cards and had six cards from the Washington Senators. He also had five cards each from the Philadelphia Athletics and Detroit Tigers.

While the T206 cards were issued from early 1909 until sometime in 1911—the year when the American Tobacco Company trust was broken up by the government—it is worth noting that in this instance we are dealing with a specific subset of the cards collected by one young boy. To estimate the boundary dates of Ted Edison's hobby, we began with Walter Corson's 1962 series-date estimates which indicated the likely earliest starting date for the 350 series as May 16, 1909, and for the 350-460 series as December 16, 1909.[3] Ted's collection includes only three of the 350-460 cards. We then consulted the *Baseball Reference* and *Baseball Almanac* major league, minor league, and managerial databases and identified sixteen cards for which the players' 1909 and 1910 team affiliations differed, which is to say, they changed teams or left baseball after the 1909 season. Of these sixteen, only two were shown on the cards with their 1910 affiliation. These included Kid Elberfeld, who was traded from New York to Washington (as shown) on December 14, 1909, and Joe Lake, who moved from New York to Salt Lake City (as shown) on December 16, 1909. While none of this is definitive with respect to the end date of the collection, when we take into consideration the fact that Ted's wallet contains a distribution date of its own, January 1, 1909, as well as contextual factors beyond the cards themselves, we are

---

3. These dates were established by Walter Corson in *The Sport Hobbyist* (Summer 1962) as reproduced by Rich Mueller, "Issue Dates of T206 Baseball Cards," *Sports Collectors Daily*, January 12, 2009, found online April 17, 2024, at https://www.sportscollectorsdaily.com/issue-dates-of-t206-baseball-cards/.

comfortable in estimating the probable starting point of the collecting period as the summer or fall of 1909, with a likely duration of several months to a year. We do not believe it likely that the collection period extended into 1911.

Given that the cards in the collection were likely from 1909 into late 1910, Ted was collecting when the New York Giants were a first-division team but failed to win the pennant. In 1909, the Pittsburgh Pirates defeated the Detroit Tigers in the World Series. The Giants finished third, behind the Pirates and Cubs. In 1910, the Philadelphia Athletics defeated the Chicago Cubs in the World Series. The Giants finished a distant second. In 1911, the Giants finally made it to the World Series again but lost to the Philadelphia Athletics. Perhaps the various World Series teams during these years were a draw for Ted. He did collect a number of Athletics, Cubs, Tigers, and Pirates cards. The Hall of Famers seem to be concentrated here, including Bender, Brown, Chance, Cobb, and Jennings.

Another curious angle to Ted's accumulation is his potential interest in the event known as "Merkle's Boner," which happened on September 23, 1908. With Cubs pitcher Jack Pfiester on the mound, Fred Merkle, a rookie on the New York Giants, failed to advance to second base on what should have been a game-winning walk-off hit by Al Bridwell for the Giants against the Cubs.[4] Moose McCormick had run in from third to home with what appeared to be the winning run, but the rookie Merkle, the youngest player in the American League at 19, just turned and headed for the clubhouse as the enthusiastic New York fans filled the field. Cubs first baseman/manager Frank Chance or second baseman Johnny Evers (depending on the account) noticed that Merkle did not advance and called for the ball from the outfield. Having retrieved it from a fan, center fielder Solly Hofman tossed it to second base, where the umpire declared the force out. This wiped out the winning run and led to a tied game. Two weeks later, the Cubs won the makeup game and the pennant. Was Ted at this game? Certainly, it was all the talk in the papers. Ted kept cards of Merkle, McCormick, Pfiester, and Chance,

---

4. "Blunder Costs Giants Victory," *New York Times*, September 24, 1908, p. 7.

who were directly involved in the play. He also had cards for Donlin, Mathewson, and Seymour, who played in the game. Lastly, he had Mordecai Brown's card—the winner of the makeup game on the final day of the season, defeating Mathewson for the pennant. It was centerfielder Seymour's lost fly in the sun that cost that one.

While we can never know what Ted was thinking at the time, these cards are a snapshot of a moment in baseball history and likely illustrate the interests, hopes, and dreams of a young fan. They also represent moments in time of 58 professional baseball careers of rising stars, north stars, shooting stars, wannabes, and never-weres.

THE CARDS AND THE PLAYERS[1]

1. Except as noted, the biographical information in this section is extracted and amalgamated primarily from the following sources: *Baseball Almanac*, found online March 18, 2024, at https://www.baseball-almanac.com/players/ballplayer.shtml; *Baseball Reference*, found online March 18, 2024, at https://www.baseball-reference.com; the Biography Project of the Society for American Baseball Research, found online March 18, 2024, at https://sabr.org; and T206 Museum's listing of T206 cards issued, found online March 18, 2024, at http://www.t206museum.com/ch_varlt.html. Here and in the profiles that follow the position and team affiliation of each player at the time the baseball card was produced are shown in **boldface**.

LEON KESSLING "RED" AMES

AMES, N. Y. NAT'L

RED AMES was born in Warren, Ohio, in 1882. He was a right-hand throwing, switch-hitting **pitcher** whose seventeen-year major league career saw him in the uniforms of the **Giants** (1903–1913), Reds (1913–1915), Cardinals (1915–1919), and Phillies (1919). He pitched more than 3000 innings, won 183 games, and had a lifetime ERA of 2.63. Ames was most notable for his curveball, which *Sporting Life* once described as perhaps the most difficult to catch in professional baseball. He was not, however, known for his pinpoint control. Throughout his career, Ames walked more than 1000 batters, and in 1905, he set an enduring major league record by throwing thirty wild pitches. He also had a hard-earned reputation as a hard-luck pitcher. On Opening Day 1909, he threw nine hitless innings against Brooklyn and kept the game scoreless through twelve, then lost in the thirteenth. On Opening Day 1910, he held Boston hitless through seven, and on Opening Day 1911, he held the Phillies hitless through six and scoreless through eight, but he lost both of those games as well. Ames died in 1936 and is buried in Warren, Ohio.

CARD DETAILS: Hands above head pose, Sweet Caporal, 350 series, factory 30. One of three variants.

John Joseph Anderson

JOHN ANDERSON was born in Norway in 1873. At six-foot-two and 180 pounds, he was among the physically biggest ballplayers of his era. He was a man of many nicknames: "Honest John" for his temperament, "Long John" and "Big John" for his height, and the "Swedish Apollo" for his good looks and muscular build. Over fourteen years as an **outfielder** and **first baseman** he played for eight different teams, the Brooklyn Bridegrooms (1894-1898), Washington Senators (1898-1899, 1905–1907), Brooklyn Superbas (1899), Milwaukee Brewers (1901), St. Louis Browns (1902–1903), New York Highlanders (1904–1905), and the Chicago White Sox (1908), before finishing his career with the **Providence Grays** of the Eastern League in 1909. Anderson was a speedy runner and an impactful hitter, often batting cleanup or fifth in the lineup, but early in his career, he was a poor fielder, especially in the outfield, where his fielding percentage dipped as low as .778 and .882 before showing later improvement. He is one of the few players to have a play named after him, though he probably would have preferred otherwise. In 1903, Anderson tried to steal second base with the bases loaded and was, of course, called out since the base was already occupied. That play has been known ever since as a "John Anderson." Upon retirement from the game, Anderson joined the police force in Worcester, Massachusetts. He died there in 1949.

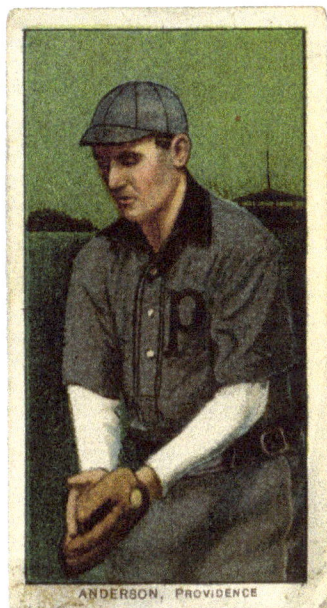

CARD DETAILS: Sweet Caporal, 350 series, factory 30.

CHARLES ALBERT "CHIEF" BENDER

BENDER, PHILA. AMER

CHIEF BENDER was a Native American born in Crow Wing County, Minnesota, in 1884. He was a right-handed **pitcher** who spent most of his sixteen-year career with the **Philadelphia Athletics** (1903–1914), then moved on to the Baltimore Terrapins of the Federal League (1915) and the Phillies (1916–1917) before returning for one cameo appearance with the White Sox in 1925. The nickname "Chief" was commonly applied to any Native American ballplayer of that day. Bender's strikeout to walks ratio of roughly 2.4:1, his ERA of 2.46, and his winning percentage of .625 marked him as one of the star pitchers of the Deadball Era and earned him a place in the Hall of Fame. A graduate of the Carlisle Indian School in Pennsylvania, Bender suffered from poor health and alcoholism but nevertheless compiled an impressive career record and earned a reputation for pitching well under pressure. After being released by the Phillies after the 1917 season, Bender worked in a shipyard during World War I, then moved to the minor leagues as a player/manager and coached baseball for several years at the U.S. Naval Academy. He later coached and scouted for several major league teams. Bender died in Philadelphia in 1954.

CARD DETAILS: Pitching pose, trees in background, Sweet Caporal, 350 series, factory 30. One of three variants.

CHARLES CARL "HEINIE" BERGER

BERGER, CLEVELAND

HEINIE BERGER was born in La Salle, Illinois, in 1882. His career as a major league **pitcher** was a brief one, lasting just four years, all of them spent with the **Cleveland Naps** (1907–1910). The nickname Heinie was commonly applied to players of German extraction at the time. Berger, a right-hander, pitched in 90 games, including 68 starts, winning 32 while losing 29. In 1909, Berger started 29 games and led the league in two categories: he struck out an average of 5.9 batters per nine innings, and he threw thirteen wild pitches. Following the 1910 season, Berger went on to play minor league baseball in Columbus, Mobile, and Nashville before retiring from the game in 1915. Berger died in Cleveland in 1954.

CARD DETAILS: Tolstoi, factory 30.

DAVID LEONARD BRAIN

BRAIN, BUFFALO

DAVE BRAIN was born in Hereford, England, in 1879. Though primarily a **third baseman**, he also played shortstop and in the outfield. Throughout a seven-year career, playing five games for the American League Chicago White Sox (1901) before the consolidation of the major leagues under the National Agreement, then wearing a series of National League uniforms, including the Cardinals (1903–1905), Pirates (1905), Boston Doves (1906–1907), Reds (1908), and Giants (1908). In 1909, he moved to the **Buffalo Bisons** of the Class A Eastern League, where he finished his baseball career the following year. On the infield, he alternated between making spectacular plays and committing errors—247 of the latter in his 675 games in the majors, or more than one in every three games. Against this, he could be a solid offensive player, hitting ten home runs for Boston in 1907 to lead the league. In 1905, Brain hit three triples in a single ballgame—twice—the only major leaguer ever to accomplish that feat. Off the field, Brain was known for his contract disputes with management. When he retired, Brain moved to California, where he worked for National Biscuit Company and then Standard Oil. He died in Whittier, California, in 1959.

CARD DETAILS: Sweet Caporal, 350 series, factory 30.

Mordecai Peter Centennial "Three Finger" Brown

M. BROWN, CHICAGO NAT'L

As one of his given names might suggest, MORDECAI BROWN was born in the Centennial year of 1876 in Nyesville, Indiana. His Hall of Fame career as a **pitcher** was spent mainly with the **Cubs** (1903–1912, 1916), with back-end stints with the Reds (1913), Brooklyn Tip-Tops (1914), St. Louis Terriers (1914) and the Chicago Whales (1915), the latter three being teams in the Federal League. With his $10,000 salary in 1914, twice what he had earned with Cincinnati the year before, Brown provides a perfect example of the tactics the Federal League employed to gain acceptance as the third major league. Over his career, he compiled 239 wins against 130 losses, with an ERA of just 2.06 over more than 3000 innings pitched. The right-hander was known for his battles against Giants Hall of Famer Christy Mathewson. Brown earned his nickname as a child, the result of catching his index finger in a piece of farm equipment, then a fall that broke two more digits. This left him with a bent middle finger, a paralyzed little finger, and a stump—a collective deformity that let him put unusual movement on his pitches, once described by Ty Cobb as the most difficult he'd ever tried to hit. Later in life, Brown operated a service station in Terre Haute, Indiana, where he died in 1948.

CARD DETAILS: CHICAGO on uniform, Sweet Caporal, 350 series, factory 30. One of three variants.

ALBERT WILLIAM BURCH

BURCH, BROOKLYN

AL BURCH, born in Albany, New York, in 1883, spent his major league career with the St. Louis Cardinals (1906–1907) and the **Brooklyn Superbas** (1907–1911). He was primarily an **outfielder**, playing 325 games in center field and around 120 each in the corner positions. He had far and away his best year at the plate in 1909, when he hit for a .271 average with 26 extra-base hits and 30 RBI, all of which points to his having been a very average batsman. In 1906, Burch was involved in an unusual double play. With a runner on first in a game against Boston, Burch came to the plate. He lined a ball back at the pitcher, striking him on the temple and knocking him to the ground. The ball bounced off his head and back toward the Boston catcher, who fielded it on the fly and threw to first, catching the runner off the bag on his way to second.[2] Burch died in Brooklyn, New York, in October 1926, two days short of his forty-third birthday.

CARD DETAILS: Fielding pose, Sweet Caporal, 350 series, factory 30. One of two variants.

---

2. L. Robert Davids, "A Unique Double Play," *Baseball Research Journal*, October 16, 1983, found online March 17, 2024, at https://sabr.org/journal/article/a-unique-double-play/.

FREDERICK DUFF BURCHELL

BURCHELL, BUFFALO

FRED BURCHELL was born in Perth Amboy, New Jersey, in 1879. A left-handed **pitcher**, he had a short major league career of just four years with two teams, the Phillies (1903) and the Boston Americans/Red Sox (1907–1909), while playing in the interim for Class A Baltimore in the Eastern League between 1904 and 1907. With 92 bases on balls, 13 wild pitches, and 16 hit batters in a mere 49 games over his major league tenure, it is fair to say he was not known for his control, though he did strike out 32 more batters than he walked. Burchell opened the 1909 season down in the minors at Class A **Buffalo**, where he won six games and lost nine before being called back up to the Red Sox. In 1910, it was back to Buffalo and on to Montreal, also in the Eastern League, though he did not play a game for either that year. After another season in Montreal in 1911, he moved to Syracuse of the Class B New York State League as a player/manager between 1912 and 1914. In 1926, Burchell returned to baseball for a single season as manager of the Newark Bears of the Class AA International League. He died in Jordan, New York, in 1951.

CARD DETAILS: Sweet Caporal, 350 series, factory 30.

SAMUEL HOWARD "RED" CAMNITZ

CAMNITZ, PITTSBURG

RED CAMNITZ, a right-handed **pitcher**, was born in Covington, Kentucky, in 1881. He spent the greater part of his career with the **Pittsburgh Pirates** (1904–1913) before moving on to the Phillies (1913) and the Pittsburgh Rebels (1914) of the Federal League. In 1909, when the Pirates became World Champions, Camnitz was the ace of their pitching staff, with a record of 25-6 and an ERA of 1.62, all heralded by an Opening Day shutout against the Reds, one of six goose eggs he posted that season. His younger brother Harry joined him very briefly on the staff that year, pitching four innings. While Camnitz had been instrumental in getting the Pirates into the 1909 World Series, he pitched poorly in those games. That was a harbinger of sorts, as his career trended downward from that point forward. His ERA, for example, doubled the following season when he won only 12 games. Unlike some of his contemporaries, after his jump to the Federal League and the later collapse of that circuit, Camnitz was never able to catch on with another ballclub. He retired to Louisville, where he worked in auto sales for four decades before he died in 1960.

CARD DETAILS: Arms at side pose, Tolstoi, factory 30. One of three variants.

PETER FRANCIS CASSIDY

By the time this T206 card was published, **PETE CASSIDY** had been out of the major leagues for a decade and was in the very last year of a lengthy minor league career. Born in Wilmington, Delaware, in 1873, Cassidy played in 101 major league games with three separate teams across two years, including Louisville (1896), Brooklyn (1899), and Washington (1899). He was primarily a **first baseman** but also saw service on the left side of the infield. In contrast, he spent fifteen seasons in the minors before, in the middle of, and following his days in the National League, including stops with the Johnstown Buckskins of the New York State League (Class B), Grand Rapids Gold Bugs of the Western League (Class A), Minneapolis Millers of the Western League, Newark Colts of the Atlantic League (Class B), Providence Clamdiggers/Grays and Jersey City Skeeters of the Eastern League (Class A), Wilmington Peaches of the Tri-State League (Class B), and finally the **Baltimore Orioles** of the Eastern League, where he played his last 86 games in 1909. The Jersey City team he joined in 1903 was one of the greatest minor league teams of all time, posting a record of 92-33 and a winning percentage of .736, which still ranks as the seventh-best in minor league history. He also managed the Wilmington team in 1907 and 1911. He died in Wilmington in 1929.

CARD DETAILS: Sweet Caporal, 350 series, factory 30.

FRANK LEROY "THE PEERLESS LEADER" CHANCE

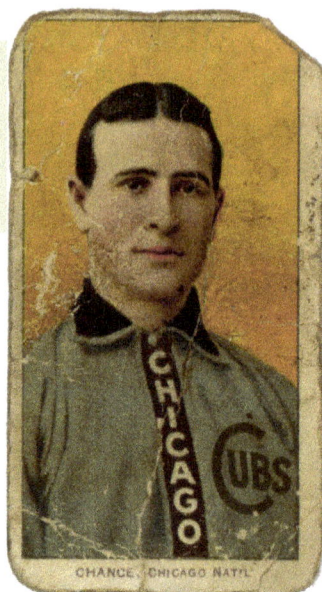

FRANK CHANCE, born in Fresno, California, in 1876, was signed by the **Cubs** as a backup catcher in 1898, reluctantly moved to **first base** in 1905, and never looked back on what became a Hall of Fame career. Chance stayed with the Cubs for fifteen years and was the team's player/manager from the middle of the 1905 season until he moved to the Yankees (also as player/manager, though he played in only 13 games during that stint) for the 1913 and 1914 seasons, after which he retired. He entered baseball lore as the anchor of the lyrical double-play combination of Tinker to Evers to Chance. Chance was a career .297 hitter with 20 home runs, a respectable total for the Dead Ball Era. He also maintained a fielding percentage of .987, committing only 135 errors in 17 seasons at first base, a remarkable accomplishment in itself. Known variously as Husk or The Peerless Leader, Chance was also famous for his tenacious play, temper, and use of foul language. He routinely knocked over opponents when running the bases, once physically assaulted an opposing pitcher, and even tossed beer bottles at rowdy opposing fans. He was known to fine his own players for shaking hands with their opponents following a game. Chance was inclined to crowd the plate during his at-bats and was hit by pitches 137 times, including several times in the head. Indeed, he developed blood clots in his brain from the beanings, and it was during his hospital recovery from the resultant brain surgery that the Cubs fired him after an argument with team owner Charles Webb Murphy. He died in Los Angeles in 1924.

CARD DETAILS: Portrait with yellow background, Sweet Caporal, 350 series, factory 30. One of three variants.

HAROLD HOMER "PRINCE HAL" CHASE

CHASE, N. Y. AMER.

HAL CHASE was born in Los Gatos, California, in 1883. He played **first base** for fifteen years in the majors, beginning with the **New York Highlanders**/Yankees (1905–1913) and moving to the White Sox (1913–1914), jumping to the Buffalo Buffeds of the Federal League (1914–1915), then on to the National League with the Reds (1916–1918), and finally the Giants (1919). Throughout his career, he hit 57 home runs, though twenty of those were hit during his brief stint in the Federal League. Chase was graceful and personally charming and quickly developed a reputation as one of the game's premier first basemen, in many ways redefining expectations for that position. But he was also notoriously corrupt and disloyal, jumping from team to team and league to league and generally leaving in his wake one kind of scandal or another, including gambling and throwing games. Chase retired to Arizona in 1920, where he played semi-pro baseball and recruited several teammates from the 1919 Black Sox team, and even once admitted he had known about that fix in advance. His later years were characterized by poverty and poor health. Hal Chase died in Colusa, California, in 1947.

CARD DETAILS: Holding cup pose, Sweet Caporal, 460 series, factory 30. One of five variants.

WILLIAM EDWARD "BILL" CLANCY

CLANCY, BUFFALO

Born in Redfield, New York, in 1879, **BILL CLANCY** played a single season of major league ball with the Pittsburgh Pirates (1905). But he did have a much longer minor league career, including stops with the Worcester Hustlers (1902) and the Montreal Royals/Worcester Riddlers (1903) of the Class A Eastern League, the Oakland Oaks of the Class A Pacific Coast League (1904), at the time a so-called "outlaw" league because it did not choose to participate in the nascent National Agreement, then back to Montreal (1904), and on to the Rochester Bronchos (1905, 1906–1907, 1908), **Buffalo Bisons** (1908, 1909), and Baltimore Orioles (1910), all once again of the Eastern League, and finally, to the Fort Wayne Brakes and Railroaders (1911–1912) of the Class B Central League. Clancy was a solid fielding **first baseman** but a weak hitter. Clancy was recruited by the Cubs in 1904 but refused to report, preferring to remain in the minor leagues, which had two effects. First, it put his career in jeopardy at a time when many of the contracting rules in baseball were in flux. Second, it led reporters to question his courage, even going so far as to label him a chicken. His one season with the Pirates ended abruptly when owner Barney Dreyfuss caught him drinking. Clancy died in Oriskany, New York, in 1948.

CARD DETAILS: Sweet Caporal, 350 series, factory 30. Some cards misspell this player's name as "Clancey."

WILLIAM JOHNSTON "DERBY DAY BILL" CLYMER

CLYMER, COLUMBUS

BILL CLYMER was born in Philadelphia in 1872 or 1873 and played a single major league season with the Philadelphia Athletics of the American Association (1891). He came to the A's from the Lebanon Cedars of the Class A Eastern Association, then went on to play with Portland of the Class B New England League (1892-1893), the Buffalo Bisons of the Class A Eastern League (1894-1897), the Rochester Patriots/Ottawa Wanderers, also of the Eastern League (1898), the Wilkes-Barre Coal Barons of the Class A Atlantic League (1899), the Kansas City Blues of the Class A Western League (1899), the Toronto Canucks of the Eastern League (1900), then back to Wilkes-Barre (1900), back to Buffalo (1901), on to the Louisville Colonels of the American Association (1902–1903), thence to the Columbus Senators of the American Association (1904–1908), and back to Wilkes-Barre in 1911, before appearing in one game for the Newark Bears of the AA-level International League in 1922. It is fair to say that Derby Day Bill Clymer was a much-traveled player. But he was also a manager for many of these teams as well as the Scranton Miners of the New York-Pennsylvania League, ending his managing career in 1932. And he was good at it. His managerial record was 2,122-1,762, making him the second minor league manager to pass the 2,000-win mark. He currently stands ninth on the all-time list. His T206 card is somewhat unique in that he was not a player, but rather only the **manager** of the **Columbus** team represented there. As for his major league career? He played shortstop in three games for the Athletics, going hitless with two strikeouts in eleven at-bats. Bill Clymer died in Philadelphia in 1936.

CARD DETAILS: Sweet Caporal, 350 series, factory 30.

TYRUS RAYMOND "THE GEORGIA PEACH" COBB

COBB, DETROIT

Born in Narrows, Georgia, in 1886, **TY COBB**, known as The Georgia Peach, became one of the best-known and most remembered players in the history of the game. He was a member of the first "class" honored in the Hall of Fame when it opened in 1939. Playing for the **Detroit Tigers** from 1905 through 1926, mainly in **center field**, and as a corner outfielder for the Philadelphia Athletics in 1927–1928, Cobb distinguished himself as the premier hitter of his era, compiling more than 4,000 hits, a lifetime batting average of .366, and nearly 2000 RBI over his 24-year career. At the same time, he distinguished himself as one of the most aggressive and temperamental players ever to don a major league uniform. Cobb was known to get into scrapes frequently, both on and off the field, and was unpopular among his peers and highly controversial as both the victim and an accused perpetrator of various fixes. In recent years, baseball historians have begun to take a second look at Cobb, who was a very complex man. The son of educators and a savvy investor, he used his wealth to provide scholarships to students, build a hospital, and even contribute anonymously to support aging ex-ballplayers in difficult circumstances. As that would suggest, Cobb was financially secure in his later life. He died in Atlanta in 1961.

CARD DETAILS: Portrait with red background, Sweet Caporal, 350 series, factory 30. One of five variants.

WILLIAM HENRY "BIG BILL" DINNEEN

DINEEN, ST. LOUIS AMER.

BILL DINNEEN was born in Syracuse, New York, in 1876. A six-foot-one right-handed **pitcher**, he played four years in the National League with the Washington Senators (1898-1899) and the Boston Beaneaters (1900–1901), then finished his career in the American League with the Boston Americans (1902–1907) and the **St. Louis Browns** (1907–1909). Dinneen compiled a record of 170 wins against 177 losses, reaching his peak in 1904 when he went 23-14. His main claim to fame probably came in the inaugural 1903 World Series, when he won three games for the Boston squad, including the first two shutouts in World Series play, and notched 28 strikeouts. During his career up to 1906, Dinneen was a genuine "innings-eater" in today's parlance, pitching between 218 and 371 frames annually. He had a lifetime ERA of 3.01. Following his career as a player, Dinneen joined the American League as an umpire, a position he maintained for an additional 28 years. He was behind the plate when Babe Ruth hit his historic sixtieth home run in 1927 and again for the first All-Star game in 1933. At age 77, Dinneen returned to the mound as a pitcher, throwing out the ceremonial first pitch of Game 2 of the 1953 World Series. Big Bill Dinneen died in Syracuse in 1955.

CARD DETAILS: Sweet Caporal, 350 series, factory 30. Dinneen's name is misspelled on this card.

MICHAEL JOSEPH "TURKEY MIKE" DONLIN

DONLIN, N. Y. NAT'L

MIKE DONLIN was born in Peoria, Illinois, in 1878. Over his twelve-year major league career, he played for the St. Louis Perfectos (1899), the Cardinals (1900), the Baltimore Orioles (1901), the Cincinnati Reds (1902–1904), the **New York Giants** (1904–1906, 1908, 1911), the Boston Rustlers (1911), and the Pittsburgh Pirates (1912), before returning to the Giants in 1914. In 1909, when this card was produced, the versatile **outfielder** was out of baseball, choosing instead a career as a playwright and actor. Together with his stage star wife, Mabel Hite, Donlin wrote a play, *Stealing Home*, that opened to acclaim on Broadway in October 1908, though his acting was less well received. The couple toured with the play for about two years, then followed up with a play that lasted mere weeks. Donlin returned to the diamond but at that point, was clearly past his prime. Throughout all of these adventures, Turkey Mike had a well-earned reputation as a man about town, and not in a good way. He was caught binge drinking, urinating in public, and accosting two chorus girls, for the last of which he was sentenced to six months in prison. When Hite died of cancer, Donlin married the niece of a vaudeville couple and once again took to the stage, after which he headed to Hollywood to begin a new career as a screen actor. Along the way, Donlin collected many famous friends, among them Jack Dempsey, Winston Churchill, Albert Einstein, and John Barrymore. Turkey Mike Donlin lived large; he died in Hollywood, California, in 1933.

CARD DETAILS: Seated pose, Sweet Caporal, 350 series, factory 30. One of three variants.

John Joseph Dunn

JACK DUNN was born in Meadville, Pennsylvania, in 1872. A right-handed **pitcher**, he played for Brooklyn (1897–1900), the Phillies (1900–1901), the Baltimore Orioles (1901), and the Giants (1902–1904). He compiled a record of 64-59, with an ERA of 4.11 over 142 games. In 1905, Dunn dropped down to the Class A Eastern League, playing first with the Providence Clamdiggers (1905–1906) before returning to the Orioles, themselves no longer in the majors (1909–1911, and for one game in 1919 when the Eastern League reinvented itself as the Class AA International League). Dunn made his real mark as a manager, beginning with his move to Providence and continuing with **Baltimore** until 1928. His 1920 AA Orioles had a record of 109 and 44. With an assist from Philadelphia Athletics' owner Connie Mack, Dunn eventually purchased the Orioles franchise from Ned Hanlon, for whom he had played and managed, in 1909, the year this card was published. It was Dunn who, in 1914, signed an unknown pitcher to a contract with the Orioles. To obtain that player's release from St. Mary's Industrial School, Dunn had to become his legal guardian. The player, of course, was George Herman Ruth, and Dunn's action changed baseball forever.

CARD DETAILS: Sweet Caporal, 350 series, factory 30.

JOSEPH EDWARD "BULLETS" DUNN

DUNN, BROOKLYN

Joe Dunn was born in Springfield, Ohio, in 1885. In a brief major league career spanning just two years (1908–1909), he was a **catcher** for the **Brooklyn Superbas**. In that time, he played in just thirty games, including three in which he was only a pinch hitter. A highlight was his very first at-bat, in which he hit a double off Christy Mathewson. It was one of fifteen total hits he compiled on his way to a lifetime batting average of .169. It is noteworthy, however, that Dunn also played eighteen seasons in the minor leagues from 1905 through 1926, including stops at every level from Class D to Class AA. Along the way, he wore the uniforms of the Terre Haute Hottentots, the Cairo (Illinois) Giants, the Roanoke Tigers, the Columbia (South Carolina) Gamecocks, the Sumter Game Cocks, Darlington (moniker unknown), the Evansville River Rats, the Mobile Sea Gulls, the Atlanta Crackers, the Dallas Giants, the Springfield (Ohio) Reapers, the Salt Lake City Bees, the Bloomington Bloomers, the Evansville Little Evas, and the Elmira Colonels. Perhaps it's a wonder he had time to stop for a cup of coffee in Brooklyn. From 1915 onward, Dunn served, or doubled, as a manager for several of these teams as well as the Birmingham Barons, and also served as a scout, owner, or general manager, finally retiring from the game in 1932. He worked from that time forward as a district manager for Shell Oil until 1944, when he died in the city of his birth, Springfield, Ohio.

CARD DETAILS: Sweet Caporal, 350 series, factory 30.

JAMES HENRY "SUNNY JIM" DYGERT

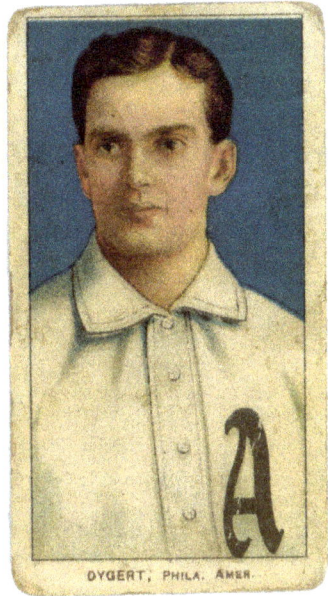

DYGERT, PHILA. AMER.

Jimmy Dygert was born in Utica, New York, in 1884. Weighing in at around 160 pounds, he was a smallish right-handed **pitcher** by today's standards and even by those of the Deadball Era. Perhaps for that reason, he relied heavily on his spitball. He spent his entire six-season major league career with the **Philadelphia Athletics** (1905–1910), where he garnered 57 wins against 49 losses. Dygert was first called up from the minors in September 1905, taking the place of the injured Rube Waddell, and in his first game notched a victory against a future legend, Cy Young. His best year was 1907 when he went 21-8 with an ERA of 2.34. In 1909, he spent much of his time in the bullpen, starting just 13 of the 32 games in which he appeared. Dygert had some issues with his control, issuing 383 bases on balls, hitting 52 batters, and throwing 33 wild pitches over 986 innings pitched. The A's played in two World Series during his years with the team, but Dygert did not pitch at all in either series. Dygert stayed in baseball for several years after 1910, playing with the Class A (and later AA) Baltimore Orioles and New Orleans Pelicans, the Beaumont Oilers of the Class B Texas League, and lastly, the Chattanooga Lookouts of the Class A Southern League, where he concluded his career in 1913. After baseball, Sunny Jim Dygert worked in the building trades in New Orleans and died there in 1936.

CARD DETAILS: Sweet Caporal, 350 series, factory 30.

Norman Arthur "Kid" Elberfeld

ELBERFELD, WASHINGTON

KID ELBERFELD, also known as The Tabasco Kid, was born in Pomeroy, Ohio, in 1875. An infielder who mainly alternated between **shortstop** and **third base**, he played in the majors for fourteen years, including stints with the Phillies (1898), the Reds (1899), the Tigers (1902–1903), the New York Highlanders (1903–1909), the **Senators** (1910–1911), and, after a hiatus with Montgomery and Chattanooga of the Southern Association, the Brooklyn Robins (1914). He then went on to a sixteen-year managerial career, mostly with teams in the Southern Association. Elberfeld had a respectable career batting average of .271 and stole 213 bases, 66 of those in his final three years. The Tabasco Kid was known, as the name suggests, for his hot temper, fearlessness, aggressiveness, and scrappy—some said dirty—style of play. In his view, what the umpire didn't see was none of the umpire's business. After his major league career ended, he moved on to playing and managing at the minor league level, where he was better at scouting young talent than preparing his players for the majors. In the 1920s, he began participating in baseball schools in the South, and in the 1940s, he ran annual baseball camps in Louisiana under the sponsorship of Coca-Cola. Among others, Elberfeld discovered or helped develop such future stars as Casey Stengel and Bill Terry. The Tabasco Kid died in Chattanooga in 1944.

CARD DETAILS: Fielding pose, Tolstoi, factory 30. One of three variants.

FREDERICK LAWRENCE JACKLITSCH

FRED JACKLITSCH was born in Brooklyn in 1876, the same year as the National League was formed. Primarily a **catcher**, but one who also played at various times in his major league career at first base, second base, shortstop, third base and in at least two outfield positions, he spent a total of thirteen seasons in major league baseball interspersed with minor league stints. He played for the **Phillies** (1900–1902, 1907–1910), the Brooklyn Superbas (1903–1904), the Yankees (1905), the Baltimore Terrapins of the Federal League (1914–1915), and the Boston Braves (1917). Jacklitsch was a solid defensive catcher and an average hitter with limited power—one who seemed to have a particular knack for hitting Phillies pitching when playing for the team's opponents (perhaps because he had caught the pitchers he was facing). Only once, in his first year at Baltimore, did he appear in more than 100 games. From 1926–1931, he served as the head baseball coach for the Rutgers University team, compiling a record of 43-42.[3] Fred Jacklitsch died in Brooklyn in 1937.

CARD DETAILS: Sweet Caporal, 350 series, factory 30.

---

3. See the 2022 Rutgers Baseball Fact Book, p. 39, found online April 3, 2024, at https://scarletknights.com/documents/2022/2/8//22Baseball_FactBook.pdf?id=16972.

HUGH AMBROSE "EEYAH" JENNINGS

Hall of Famer **HUGHIE EEYAH JENNINGS**, nicknamed for his characteristic piercing yell, was born in Pittston, Pennsylvania, in 1869, making him one of the oldest players featured in the T206 series of cards. Between 1891 and 1918—an eighteen-year baseball career—Jennings played a variety of infield positions as well as the corner outfield positions. He is pictured on this T206 card at his position in 1909,

first base. After three years with Louisville (1891–1893) in the American Association and then the National League, he played with the Baltimore Orioles (1893-1898, 1899), the Brooklyn Superbas (1899, 1900, 1903), the Phillies (1901–1902), and the **Detroit Tigers** (1907, 1909, 1912). His career batting average of .312 and slugging percentage of .406 marked him as a leading offensive player of the day, while his 287 times hit by a pitch—an all-time career record—including 202 times during five years with the Orioles (51 in 1896 alone, and thrice in one game three separate times)—simply marked him. For a time, he was the premier shortstop in the game and finished second in the race for the 1896 batting title with an average of .401. He was **manager** of the Tigers from 1907 to 1920, during which time the team won three pennants. In this role, he was the man in charge of wrangling the pugnacious rookie and then veteran Ty Cobb. Beginning in 1899, he studied law at Cornell in exchange for managing the school's baseball team and later became a successful trial lawyer in Scranton, Pennsylvania, a savvy investor, and a director of several banks. After a period of declining health, he died in Scranton in 1928.

CARD DETAILS: Right hand up pose, Sweet Caporal, 350 series, factory 30. One of three variations.

WALTER PERRY "BIG TRAIN" JOHNSON

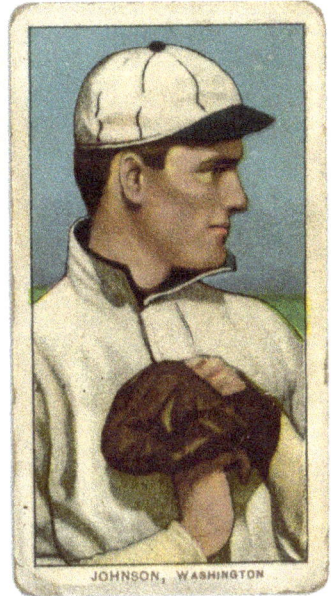

JOHNSON, WASHINGTON

WALTER JOHNSON, a member of the first "class" of five inductees to the Hall of Fame, was born in Humboldt, Kansas, in 1887. Over a twenty-one-year career with the **Washington Senators**, the six foot one inch two hundred pound **pitcher** started 666 games, ending with a record of 417 wins against 279 losses while playing for a team that was, in the immortal words of Charles Dryden, "first in war, first in peace, and last in the American League." We should remember, though, that Dryden coined that line in 1904, but Johnson did not join the club until three years later. Unusual even among the biggest stars of the era, Johnson was a one-team player, staying with the Senators from 1907 through his retirement in 1927. The Big Train was the American League's MVP twice, in 1913 and 1924, and led the league in ERA five times, in wins six times, in strikeouts seven times, in innings pitched five times, and in shutouts seven times. He still holds the major league record in that last category. Johnson won twenty or more games twelve times, including in ten successive seasons from 1910 to 1919, and won more than thirty games twice. Oddly, the year he was pictured on this T206 card, 1909, his third in the majors, was his worst; he posted a record of 13-25 despite maintaining an ERA of 2.22. It is fair to say that Walter Johnson was one of the most impactful players in the history of professional baseball. Afterward, he managed teams in Newark, Washington, and Cleveland until 1935, then retired to his farm in Maryland, serving for a time as a county commissioner. He died in Washington, D.C., in 1946.

CARD DETAILS: Hands at chest pose, Sweet Caporal, 350 series, factory 30. One of two variations.

DAVID JEFFERSON "KANGAROO" JONES

JONES, DETROIT

DAVY JONES, known as Kangaroo because of his penchant for jumping from one team to another by finding loopholes in his contracts and later because he was among the players who jumped from the American or National Leagues to the upstart Federal League in 1914, was born in Cambria, Wisconsin, in 1880. An **outfielder**, mainly in the corners, Jones played for the Milwaukee Brewers/St. Louis Browns (1901–1902) of the American League in the years just before the National Agreement, then for the Chicago Cubs of the National League (1902–1904), the **Detroit Tigers** (1906–1912) and Chicago White Sox (1913) of the American League, and the Pittsburgh Rebels of the Federal League (1914–1915), before returning to the Tigers for one last hurrah in 1918. In 1907, Jones was the first hitter to face future Hall of Famer Walter Johnson. While with Detroit, Jones spent several years in the same outfield with Ty Cobb, with whom he seemed to get along well and, by some accounts, whose behavior he sometimes instigated. Early in his career, he founded a chain of drug stores that his brother ran, and upon retiring, he obtained a degree in pharmacy from the University of Southern California, then returned to Michigan, where he worked in his drug stores for four decades. Jones died in Mankato, Minnesota, in 1972.

CARD DETAILS: Tolstoi, factory 30.

JOSEPH JAMES "HANDSOME JOE" KELLEY

Handsome **JOE KELLEY** was born in Cambridge, Massachusetts, in 1871 and began his major league career close to home with the Boston Beaneaters in 1891. His playing career as an outfielder and first baseman lasted seventeen years and included stops with Pittsburgh (1892), Baltimore (1892-1898, 1902), the Brooklyn Superbas (1899–1901), Cincinnati (1902–1906), and the Boston Doves (1908). In 1909, when this card was produced, Kelley was the **manager** of the **Toronto Maple Leafs** of the Class A Eastern League. He returned to that position in 1912–1914 when the team was playing in the Class AA International League. During his playing days, Kelley was a potent hitter, with a career batting average of .317, a slugging percentage of .451, 194 triples and 65 home runs, all significant accomplishments in the Deadball Era, significant enough to merit selection to the Hall of Fame. With Baltimore, he was known as the Kingpin of the Orioles, though over the years, he had a complex relationship with the team due in part to the decision of owner Ned Hanlon to move, lock, stock, and star players, to Brooklyn, where the team was renamed the Superbas. When his managerial time in Toronto came to an end, Kelley served for a time as chief scout for the New York Yankees. He eventually retired to Baltimore, where he was active in Democratic Party politics, and where he died in 1943.

CARD DETAILS: Sweet Caporal, 350 series, factory 30.

FRANZ OTTO "DUTCH" KNABE

OTTO KNABE was born in Carrick, Pennsylvania, in 1884. He played **second base** for a series of teams, including the Pirates (1905 and again in 1916), the **Phillies** (1907–1913), the Baltimore Terrapins of the Federal League (1914–1915), and the Cubs (1916). He was an average hitter with average power and a somewhat error-prone fielder, making more than 30 miscues in six of his ten seasons with the Phillies. In 1908 and 1913, he led the National League in the number of outs made on offense. Dutch Knabe provides another example of the incentives offered by the Federal League to attract players from its rivals. In 1913, Knabe was paid a salary of $3300 by the Phillies; in 1914 and 1915, he was paid $10,000 per year, literally three times as much, by the upstart Terrapins. We should note, however, that part of that compensation was doubtless attributable to the role he took on as manager of that short-lived team. In 1914, his charges had a respectable record of 84-70; in 1915, not so much, as the team went 47-107. Known for his sharp tongue during his playing days as much as for his talent in making a double play, Knabe later had a close brush with the Black Sox scandal. He was reportedly about to bet on the White Sox to win the World Series when a friend warned him off. He told his good friend and mentor Kid Gleason, manager of the White Sox, about the rumor, which led to a split between the two. Knabe then placed a bet on the Reds. Next thing he knew, he was himself targeted long after the fact with a charge that he had conspired with some Phillies teammates to throw a series that would impact the 1908 pennant race. In his later years, Knabe ran a tavern in Philadelphia, and it was there that he died in 1961.

CARD DETAILS: Piedmont, 350 series, factory 25.

JOSEPH HENRY LAKE

Right-handed **pitcher JOE LAKE**, born in 1881, was a native of Brooklyn, New York. Over his six years in major league baseball, he played for the New York Highlanders (1908–1909), the **St. Louis Browns** (1910–1912), and the Detroit Tigers. Lake came to the Highlanders amid high hopes based on his 25-14 record pitching for the Jersey City Skeeters of the Class A Eastern League in 1907. But he spent his career on the rosters of some generally mediocre teams, including the 1910 Browns team managed by Dutch Knabe that went 47-107, and largely as a result, he compiled a generally mediocre record, with 62 wins and 90 losses. Still, his ERA of 2.85 was certainly respectable. Lake had two winning seasons, going 14-11 for New York in 1909 and 8-7 for Detroit in 1913. He spent his final year in the game with the Minneapolis Millers of the Class AA American Association. Like many players of his era, Lake could not rely on professional baseball as his sole support. So he maintained side jobs as an electrician on the Brooklyn docks and as a teaching professional at a local golf course. Lake called Brooklyn home for his entire life and died there in 1950.

CARD DETAILS: Right hand visible pose, Sweet Caporal, 350 series, factory 30. One of three variants.

WILLIAM HERSHEL "SLOTHFUL BILL" LATTIMORE

LATTIMORE, TOLEDO

BILL LATTIMORE was born in Roxton, Texas, in 1884. He was a smallish left-handed **pitcher**, standing five foot nine and weighing in at 165 pounds. His major league career was brief. After spending some unrecorded portion of 1905 with the Paris/Hope (Arizona) Parasites of the Class D North Texas League and 1906 with the Webb City (Missouri) Gold Bugs of the Class C Western Association, Lattimore caught on with the Toledo Mud Hens of the Class A American Association in 1907. The most sought-after player in the 1907 minor league draft, he was acquired from Toledo by the Cleveland Naps in September 1907 and, in 1908, pitched in four games for the team, earning a 1-2 record and a 4.50 ERA. That was it; back to the minors. He spent 1909 at **Toledo** and 1910 with the Fort Worth Panthers of the Class C Texas League before hanging up his spikes and entering the retail clothing business in Texas. Unfortunately, Lattimore's life was as brief as his major league career. After contracting tuberculosis, he moved to the Rocky Mountains to improve his health. He died in Colorado Springs in 1919 at the age of 35. As for that nickname? It was a gift from *Sporting Life* magazine, which deemed him to have the slowest pace of play of any pitcher in the game.

CARD DETAILS: Sweet Caporal, 350 series, factory 30.

PATRICK JOSEPH "PADDY" LIVINGSTON

LIVINGSTONE, PHILA. AMER.

PADDY LIVINGSTON was born in Cleveland, Ohio, in 1880 and began his major league career with the hometown Cleveland Blues in 1901, playing in one game and registering a strikeout and a hit-by-pitch in three plate appearances. The **catcher** next caught on with the Terre Haute Hottentots (1903) and the Wheeling Stogies (1905) of the Class B Central League before returning briefly to the majors, playing in 50 games for the Cincinnati Reds in 1906. Then it was off to the Indianapolis Indians of the Class A American Association (1907–1908), followed by a slightly longer trip to "the show" with the **Philadelphia Athletics** (1909–1911) and the Cleveland Naps (1912). Then it was back to Indianapolis (1913–1914), by then a AA-level team, followed by the Sioux City Indians of the Class A Western League (1916), and a rebound to AA ball with the Milwaukee Brewers (1917). Later that season, he returned to the majors briefly, playing in seven games with the St. Louis Cardinals. Throughout his seven seasons at the highest level, Livingston played in a total of 206 games and earned a batting average that, at .209, was just barely higher. He spent the 1919 season as a bullpen catcher for the Athletics, then four decades working for the department that maintained Cleveland's bridges. He died in Cleveland in 1977 at the age of 97.

CARD DETAILS: Duplicates. Both examples are Sweet Caporal, 350 series, factory 30. The player's name is misspelled on these cards.

HARRY DONALD LORD

LORD, BOSTON AMER.

HARRY LORD was born in Porter, Maine, in 1882. A **third baseman** for much of his career, he also played all three outfield positions. Lord broke into the major leagues with the **Boston Americans/Red Sox** (1907–1910), then moved on to the Chicago White Sox (1910–1914) before jumping to the Buffalo Blues (AKA, the Buffeds) of the Federal League in 1915. He managed the Blues for part of the 1915 season, making him one of ten alumni of the 1910 Red Sox team who would go on to manage in the major leagues, but at the end of that final Federal League campaign, Lord was blacklisted by both the American and National Leagues. He continued to play for the following two years, first with the Lowell (Massachusetts) Grays (1916) and then with the Portland (Maine) Duffs (1917), both of the Class B Eastern League, serving as well in each instance as the team's manager. After one more year (1918) managing the Jersey City Skeeters of the Class AA International League, he retired from the game. Lord batted a very respectable .278 over his nine years in the majors and stole a total of 208 bases, including 43 in 1911. In 1910 he was timed running between home plate and first base at 3.4 seconds. And in one memorable game in 1909, Lord was the lead runner in a rare event, a triple steal—the one who stole home. Harry Lord had a mixed career after baseball, including ownership of a grocery store, coaching a high school baseball team, and operating a coal business. He died in Westbrook, Maine, in 1948.

CARD DETAILS: Sweet Caporal, 350 series, factory 30.

NICHOLAS
MADDOX

NICK MADDOX, a six-foot-tall right-handed **pitcher**, was born in Govanstown, Maryland, in 1886. William Kirk of the *New York American* once described him as "a well-formed youth with a face like a dried apple."[4] He spent four years in the major leagues, all of them with the **Pittsburgh Pirates** (1907–1910). His first three seasons were promising, with records of 5-1 (ERA of 0.83) as a September call-up, 23-8, and 13-8. In 1907, he threw the first no-hitter in Pirates history. He capped off his 1909 season with a complete game win in Game 3 of that year's World Series against the Detroit Tigers. Maddox had arm trouble and compiled a record of just 2-3 over twenty games the following year with an ERA that ballooned to 3.40. Just that quickly, his career in the majors was at an end. Maddox tried to hang on, first with the Kansas City Blues and Louisville of the AA American Association, then with Class A Wichita of the Western League, where he also served as manager, but by 1914, his professional playing days were over. He pitched briefly in some industrial league games into the 1920s. Starting around 1923, he worked as a maintenance man for a Pittsburgh area brewery. He died in Pittsburgh in 1954.

CARD DETAILS: Sweet Caporal, 350 series, factory 30.

---

4. Quoted in Bill James and Rob Neyer, *The Neyer/James Guide to Pitchers: An Historical Compendium of Pitching*. New York: Simon and Schuster, 2008, p. 287.

CHRISTOPHER "BIG SIX" MATHEWSON

MATHEWSON, N. Y. NAT'L

CHRISTY MATHEWSON, Big Six, was born in Factoryville, Pennsylvania, in 1880, and in 1898, enrolled at Bucknell University, where he was a forestry major and a star athlete, and where the football stadium and other campus landmarks now bear his name. He dropped out of the university in 1901 to play professional baseball full-time. During the summer of his freshman year at Bucknell, he joined the Taunton Herrings of the Class F New England League, where he compiled a record of 2-13, but the next year, he went 20-2 pitching for Norfolk in the Virginia League before being sold to the **New York Giants**, with whom he was to spend almost his entire major league playing career (1900–1916). Mathewson moved on to manage the Cincinnati Reds for three years (1916–1918), capping off his pitching career with a single appearance for the Reds in 1916, a complete-game win despite his giving up 8 earned runs. Mathewson's first year was inauspicious—a record of 0-3 with an ERA of 5.08. But in 1901, when he began full-time play, everything changed. Mathewson quickly came to be regarded as the best **pitcher** in the major leagues, winning a total of 373 games with a lifetime ERA of 2.13 and a total of 2507 strikeouts set against 848 bases on balls for a ratio of 2.96:1. He led the National League in wins four times, in ERA five times, in strikeouts five times, in shutouts four times, and more. Twice (1905, 1908) he achieved the pitching Triple Crown by leading the league in games won-lost, ERA, and strikeouts. Mathewson pitched in four World Series for the Giants in 1905, 1911, 1912, and 1913, and his three complete-game shutouts in the first of these years remain one of baseball's most iconic achievements. Adding to all of his

accomplishments on the field, baseball itself took advantage of his reputation for honesty, intelligence, and civility to enhance the image of the
game in an era of rough personalities and sometimes even rougher play.
It is little wonder, then, that Big Six was among the first class of five hon-
orees in the Hall of Fame when it opened in 1939. Though there is some
uncertainty as to the circumstances, Mathewson, along with Ty Cobb,
volunteered for the Chemical Warfare Service in 1918 during World War
I, and Mathewson was reportedly exposed to poison gas in a training
accident. He died of tuberculosis in Saranac Lake, New York, in 1925 at
the age of 45.

CARD DETAILS: Duplicates. Both examples are dark cap pose, Sweet
Caporal, 350 series, factory 30. One of three variants.

The duplicates in Ted's Wallet: Livingstone [sic], Mathewson, and Seymour.

GEORGE FLORIAN "PINCH" MCBRIDE

MCBRIDE, WASHINGTON

GEORGE MCBRIDE was born in Milwaukee, Wisconsin, in 1880. Primarily a **shortstop**, he broke in with the hometown Milwaukee Brewers in 1901, then spent three seasons in independent and Class A ball with teams in Kansas City, Milwaukee, Peoria, and St. Joseph, Missouri. In 1905–1906, he bounced between the Kansas City team in the American Association and the St. Louis Cardinals before catching on in the majors for good. McBride played for the **Washington Senators** for the next thirteen years (1908–1920), during which time he led the American League six times in double plays turned, three times in putouts by shortstops, and five times with the best fielding percentage at his position. As was typical of shortstops of that era, he was not an offensive powerhouse, with a lifetime batting average of .221 and a slugging percentage of .268. But he had a reputation as a clutch hitter, which earned him the nickname "Pinch."[5] He stole 116 bases over the years while being caught stealing only 31 times. Between 1908 and 1914, McBride played in at least 150 of the team's 154 games each season, a notable achievement for a shortstop. McBride spent one year as manager of the Washington team in 1921 but suffered a concussion when he was hit in the head by a thrown baseball during a practice session, which caused bouts of dizziness through the remainder of the season. He later coached for the Tigers before retiring from the game in 1929. He died in Milwaukee in 1973 at the age of 92.

CARD DETAILS: Sweet Caporal, 350 series, factory 30.

---

5. Tom Zappala and Ellen Zappala, The T206 Collection: The Players & Their Stories, quoted at https://www.psacard.com/cardfacts/baseball-cards/1915-16-m101-4-sporting-news/george-mcbride-115/19796, and found online April 3, 2024.

HARRY ELWOOD "MOOSE" McCORMICK

MCCORMICK, N. Y. NAT'L

MOOSE McCORMICK was born in Philadelphia in 1881. He graduated from Girard College in Philadelphia in 1898 and then attended Bucknell University, where he, like Christy Mathewson, is now enshrined in the school's sports hall of fame. McCormick was a left-handed **outfielder** and **pinch hitter** who spent five years in the majors, playing for the **Giants** (1904, 1908–1909, 1912–1913), the Pirates (1904), and the Phillies (1908), all interspersed with time spent with the York (Pennsylvania) Penn Parks of the independent Tri-State League (1905–1906) and time away from the game (1910–1911). His lifetime batting average was .286, with 1912 representing a peak as he hit .333. That year also tells the story of McCormick as a role player, as he appeared in 42 games but made only 45 plate appearances, going 13 for 39 with 6 walks. Statistics of that sort are typical of a player who comes into games as a late substitute, either to pinch hit or as a defender. McCormack was on base and scored what seemed to be the winning run in the so-called "Merkle Game," in which Fred Merkle of the Giants was called out for failing to touch second base after the run had scored. Moose followed his major league career by, among other things, coaching the baseball teams at Bucknell and West Point and writing a how-to book on coaching the sport. He was the coach of baseball instruction in an exhibition at the New York World's Fair in 1939–1940, then served in the military during World War II, returning to Bucknell as a manager of veterans housing. He died in Lewisburg, Pennsylvania, in 1962.

CARD DETAILS: Sweet Caporal, 350 series, factory 30.

John Bannerman "Larry" McLean

LARRY McLEAN, a **catcher** and occasional first baseman, was born in Fredericton, New Brunswick, Canada, in 1881. At six foot five and 228 pounds, he was among the tallest players of the Deadball Era. McLean began his career in the majors with the Boston Americans of the American League (1901), but after a year (1903) playing in the Class B New England League in Nashua, New Hampshire, he found his calling in the National League, first with the Cubs (at the end of the 1903 season), then with the Cardinals (1904), **Cincinnati** (1906–1912), the Cardinals again (1913), and finally the New York Giants (1913–1915). The peak of his career came in 1909–1912 when he appeared in at least 95 games each season. He was a solid performer behind the plate and equally reliable in the batter's box, with a career batting average of .262 and an on-base percentage of .301. He was also difficult to strike out, with a total of only 127 strikeouts in more than 2800 plate appearances over thirteen years in the majors. Twice, he led the league in the percentage of runners caught stealing. He also had a reputation as a brawler, both on the field and off, and once reportedly collared a murder suspect on the street. In addition, he was something of a drunk and was known to bounce checks; his 1910 contract included a clause under which forty percent of his pay was withheld until the season's end as a guarantee of his sobriety. He died in Boston in 1921 when he got into a dispute with the bartender at a local speakeasy, tried to jump the bar, and was shot dead.

CARD DETAILS: Sweet Caporal, 350 series, factory 30.

CARL FREDERICK RUDOLF "BONEHEAD" MERKLE

MERKLE, N. Y. NAT'L

BONEHEAD MERKLE, whose name will live forever in baseball infamy, was born in Watertown, Wisconsin, in 1888. The right-handed **first baseman** broke into the major leagues with the **New York Giants** in 1907, remaining with the team for almost ten seasons (1907–1916) before moving first to the Brooklyn Robins (1916–1917) and thence, perhaps with a sense of irony, to the Chicago Cubs (1918–1920), before appearing a few times for the New York Yankees in 1925 and 1926. Merkle had a respectable .273 lifetime batting average and hit 61 home runs over his sixteen-year career, including 12 in 1911 and 11 in 1912. On balance, he was an exceptionally good fielder, with a lifetime fielding percentage of .985; he was the least error-prone of the National League's first basemen in four seasons, 1910–1912 and 1919. Merkle played in five World Series between 1911 and 1918 with three different teams. Together, that would seem to make Merkle a memorable player based on his performance. Alas, Merkle is indeed remembered, but not for that. In 1908, the Giants, the Pirates and the Cubs were neck and neck in the pennant race when the Chicago team paid a late September visit to the Polo Grounds. In a very confusing late-game situation that we described earlier (pages 38–39), Merkle was called out for failing to reach second base, a call that led to the game being ruled a tie that, many argued, eventually cost the Giants the pennant. It was, by the rules, a bonehead play, the kind that baseball fans love to relive time and again, and Merkle, who was, in reality, a somewhat scholarly man and a voracious reader, was known for the remainder of his career as Bonehead. Fred Merkle died in Daytona Beach, Florida, in 1956.

CARD DETAILS: Fielding pose, Sweet Caporal, 460 series, factory 30. One of two variants.

JOHN TORTES "CHIEF" MEYERS

MEYERS, N. Y. NAT'L

CHIEF MEYERS, also known as Ironman, was born in Riverside, California, in 1880. He attended Dartmouth College but was discovered to have used a false diploma to gain admission. He left the university in 1906 at age 25 to join the Harrisburg Senators of the independent Tri-State League and begin his baseball career. A **catcher**, Meyers played for the **New York Giants** (1909–1915), the Brooklyn Robins (1916–1917), and the Boston Braves (1917). He was behind the plate in at least 110 games each season from 1910–1915, thus earning the Ironman sobriquet. As for the nickname Chief, that was a common and stereotypical label applied in that era to any player of Native American heritage. Meyers was a member of the Cahuilla tribe. He was also a very sophisticated man, logical and well-educated, with a quick sense of humor. Meyers had a lifetime batting average of .291 and led the National League in on-base percentage in 1912. He led all National League catchers in putouts for five years running, 1910–1914. He was consistent in the postseason as well, playing in 18 games across four World Series and batting .290. Meyers joined the Marine Corps during World War I, then kicked around the minor leagues for a couple of years before moving back to the Riverside area, where he became a police chief for the Mission Indian Agency. He died in San Bernardino, California, in 1971.

CARD DETAILS: Sweet Caporal, 460 series, factory 30.

FREDERICK FRANCIS MITCHELL

MITCHELL, TORONTO

FRED MITCHELL was born in Cambridge, Massachusetts, in 1878. His major league career was long over by 1909 when this card was produced. Fred had been a jack-of-all-trades, serving at various times as a right-handed **pitcher**, catcher, and first baseman. His major league career included stops with the Boston Americans (1901–1902), Philadelphia Athletics (1902), Philadelphia Phillies (1903–1904), and the Brooklyn Superbas (1904–1905). He attempted a comeback with the Yankees in 1910 and again with the Boston Braves in 1913. As a pitcher, he had a record of 31-50 across that period, with an ERA of 4.10. In 1903, he was second in the National League with 17 wild pitches. As a batter, he was equally medicore, hitting .210 overall, including two seasons in which he failed to top .200. As a fielder, he was adequate. Between 1906 and 1909, Mitchell was pitching and occasionally playing second base for the **Toronto Maple Leafs** of the Class A Eastern League. In addition to his encores in New York and Boston, he played for the Rochester Bronchos in 1911 and the Buffalo Bisons in 1912. In 1917, he turned to managing, steering the Cubs for four years (1917–1920) and the Boston Braves for three (1921–1923) before retiring from the professional game to serve as the baseball coach at Harvard University. In 1918, while with the Cubs, Mitchell became club president, in which post he hired his eventual successor, baseball legend Bill Veeck, Sr. Mitchell died in Newton, Massachusetts, in 1970.

CARD DETAILS: Sweet Caporal, 350 series, factory 30.

WILLIAM WALLACE NATTRESS

BILLY NATTRESS was born in Girardville, Pennsylvania, in 1878 and attended Bucknell University. Unlike most of the players featured on the T206 cards, he never played an inning in the major leagues. He did, however, have a long minor league career, lasting for some 18 years. Nattress was a **shortstop** who batted left-handed and threw right-handed. His career saw him on the rosters of the Kansas City Blues of the Class A Western League (1895), the Omaha Omahogs of the Class B Western Association (1895), the Lewiston, Maine, team in the New England League (1896), the Hagerstown Lions of the independent Cumberland Valley League (1896), the Sunbury Pirates of the unclassified Central Pennsylvania League (1896), the Newcastle (Pennsylvania) Quakers of the Class B Interstate League (1897–1900), the Ft. Wayne Railroaders of the Class A Western Association (1901), the **Buffalo Bisons** of the Class A Eastern League (1902, 1903–1909), the Columbus Senators of the independent American Association (1902), the Montreal Royals of the Eastern, and then the Class AA International League (1910–1912), and the Syracuse Stars of the Class B New York State League (1912). It would be fair to describe Billy Nattress as an itinerant baseball player—have glove; will travel. Records from some of these seasons are, at best, uneven and, at worst, unavailable, but from those that are known, Nattress had (at least) some 5900 plate appearances with 1469 hits, including 29 home runs. In the field, where records are sparser still, he appears to have been error-prone. Beyond that, little is known of his life while playing or after he retired from the game. Nattress died in Sunbury, Pennsylvania, in 1956.

CARD DETAILS: Sweet Caporal, 350 series, factory 30.

Ennis Telfair "Rebel" Oakes

OAKES, CINCINNATI

REBEL OAKES was born in Arizona, Louisiana, in 1883; his nickname is a reminder that most of the players included in the T206 card set were born less than a generation after the end of the Civil War. After starring on the football and baseball teams at the Louisiana Industrial Institute in Ruston, Oakes began his baseball career as a **center fielder** in the low minors, first with the Hattiesburg (Mississippi) Tar Heels and the Greenville (also Mississippi) Cotton Pickers of the Class D Delta and Cotton States Leagues in 1904–1905, then with the Cedar Rapids Rabbits (1906–1907) of the Class B Illinois-Indiana-Iowa League, and finally advancing to the Los Angeles Angels (1908) of the Class A Pacific Coast League. His major league debut, captured on this card, came with **Cincinnati** (1909), after which he played for the Cardinals (1910–1913) before jumping to the Pittsburgh Rebels of the Federal League for the two seasons that league survived, 1914–1915. In Pittsburgh, he was a player/manager. Once the Federal League ceased play, it was back down the hill for Oakes, to Denver of the Class A Western League in 1916–1917 (with an interim stop in Indianapolis of the Class AA American Association), then back to Mississippi, first with the Greenwood Indians and then with the Jackson Red Sox, both in the Class D Mississippi State League and both in 1921. In Denver and Jackson, Oakes again wore a second cap as team manager. In 986 major league games and some 4000 plate appearances, he batted .279. The nickname Rebel was pinned on him by a California sports writer during his season with the Angels. After baseball, Oakes pursued a career in oil exploration back home in Louisiana. He died in Rocky Springs, Louisiana, in 1948.

CARD DETAILS: Sweet Caporal, 350 series, factory 30.

JOHN ALBERT "GIANT KILLER" PFIESTER

JACK THE GIANT KILLER was born in Cincinnati, Ohio, in 1878. He earned his beanstalk-sounding nickname by throwing seven shutouts against the New York Giants on his way to a 15-5 record against them throughout his eight-year career in the National League, first with the Pirates (1903–1904) and then with the **Cubs** (1906–1911). A left-handed **pitcher** with a side-arm delivery and a deceptive move to first, Pfiester posted a career won-lost record of 71-44 with an ERA of 2.02, leading the league in the latter category with an ERA of 1.15 in 1907. He notched an average of 4.2 strikeouts per nine innings. Still, there were intervals in which he was sent back to the farm—to the Omaha Rangers twice during his tenure in Pittsburgh when he had not yet developed into the pitcher he was to become, and once to the Louisville Colonels during his last year in Chicago. He pitched in five games across four World Series for the Cubs in 1906, 1907, 1908, and 1910, winning one and losing three. Pfiester may be best remembered, though, for having been on the mound in the 1908 "Merkle Game" when Fred Merkle failed to reach second base. In that contest, Pfiester pitched a complete game while suffering from a dislocated arm. He retired from the game in 1911 but attempted a comeback of sorts with the Class A Sioux City Indians in 1916. After a poor start, he was released mid-season. Jack Pfiester died in Loveland, Ohio, in 1953.

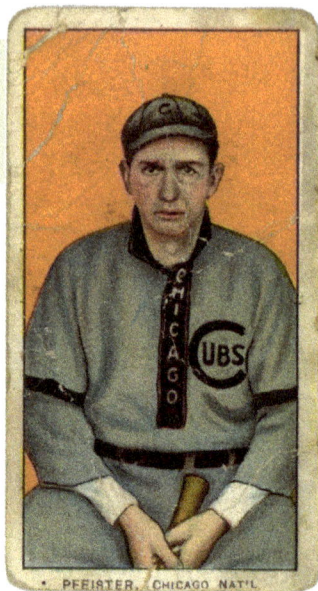

CARD DETAILS: Seated pose, Sweet Caporal, 350 series, factory 30. One of two variants.

WILLIAM PATRICK PURTELL

·PURTELL, CHICAGO AMER.

BILLY PURTELL was born in Columbus, Ohio, in 1886. A **utility infielder**, he played for the **White Sox** (1908–1910), the Red Sox (1910–1911), and the Tigers (1914). He spent more time in the minor leagues than the majors, however, including such teams as the Class A Columbus Senators (1904), the Class B Decatur Commodores (1904–1907), the Class AA Jersey City Skeeters (1912–1913), the Venice/Vernon (California) Tigers, Montreal Royals (1917), Toronto Maple Leafs (1918–1919), and Akron Buckeyes (1920); the Class B Vancouver Beavers (1921) and Columbia (South Carolina) Comers (1926); and finally the Class D Hagerstown Hubs (1928), where he also managed for part of the season. Throughout his major league career, Purtell accumulated a .227 batting average and may have been a lighter hitter than even that mark suggests. While playing in 151 games in 1910, Purtell hit only six doubles, the fewest by any player who had appeared in at least 150 games in a season. That mark remains today as the rather dubious American League record low. Purtell did manage two home runs during his major league career, one of which actually bounced off a goat and into the stands, where a fan threw the ball back onto the field. The ball was retrieved and thrown in quickly enough to hold Purtell at second base. His other "round-tripper" was equally odd: a grounder, it bounced up and struck the defending third baseman in the head, whereupon it bounced into the bleachers. Under the rules in place at the time, both hits were ruled home runs. That was baseball in the Deadball Era. Purtell died in Bradenton, Florida, in 1962.

CARD DETAILS: Sweet Caporal, 350 series, factory 30.

Newton John Randall

RANDALL, MILWAUKEE

NEWT RANDALL was born in New Lowell, Ontario, Canada, in 1880. Sources disagree on whether the **outfielder** batted from the left side of the plate or the right. In truth, it made relatively little difference because he played only one season in the majors, in 1907, split between the Chicago Cubs and the Boston Doves. He managed 71 hits in 336 at-bats for an average of .211. He came to the Cubs after having spent five seasons in the minors, with stops at Cavalier, North Dakota (1902), the Winnipeg Maroons (1903), and the Duluth White Sox (1904), all of the Class D Northern League, and the Denver Grizzlies (1905–1906) of the Class A Western League. After his brief time in "The Show," he spent another eight seasons with the Class AA **Milwaukee Brewers** (1908–1915) of the American Association and one more with the Class AA Oakland Oaks (1916) of the Pacific Coast League. Several years later, in 1923, he spent a season with the Bismarck Capitals of the Class D North Dakota League. Though not much of a batsman in the majors, Randall was a serious threat at the plate in the minors, compiling an overall average of .295. Today, we might refer to a player of Randall's abilities as a "AAAA" player—a star at all levels of the minor leagues but not good enough to stick at the major league level. Randall retired to Duluth, Minnesota, where he worked as a watchman and driver for the Minnesota Steel Company. He died there in 1955.

CARD DETAILS: Sweet Caporal, 350 series, factory 30.

WILLIAM HERMAN "GERMANY" SCHAEFER

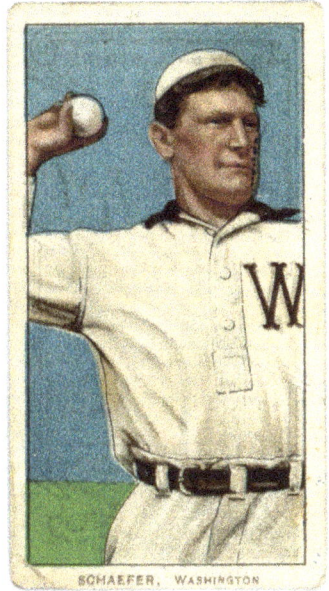

SCHAEFER, WASHINGTON

Germany Schaefer, also known as Dutch or Schaef, was born in Chicago in 1876, making him one of the oldest players featured in the T206 card set. A versatile **infielder** and occasional outfielder, and later a coach, Schaefer was known in his day as a showman who was always eager to entertain the fans. He played in the major leagues for fifteen years, wearing the uniforms of the Chicago Orphans (1901–1902), Detroit Tigers (1905–1909), **Washington Senators** (1909–1914), Newark Pepper of the Federal League (1915), New York Yankees (1916), and Cleveland Indians (1918). At the latter two stops, Schaefer served as a player/coach. His peak career years were those with Washington, where he batted .294 over six years and averaged .334 in 1911. Overall, though, his lifetime average in the major leagues was a good bit lower at .257. In two post-season appearances with Detroit in 1907–1908, he did even worse, averaging .135 in 37 at-bats against the Cubs. In 1919, John McGraw of the Giants hired Schaefer as a scout, but he died suddenly on a train in Saranac Lake, New York, before he could fill that role.

CARD DETAILS: Washington, Tolstoi, factory 30. One of two variants.

CHARLES "BOSS" SCHMIDT

Sometimes, a name tells you everything you need to know. **Catcher BOSS SCHMIDT** was born in London, Arkansas, in 1880. He played five years with the **Tigers** (1906–1911), in three of which the team earned a berth in the World Series. Schmidt was not a workhorse, playing in more than 100 games only twice during his Tigers tenure, nor was he greatly feared at the plate, with a career batting average of .243. But he filled a need for a Detroit team that was otherwise stocked with talent, and he was, in every way, a genuine tough guy. Schmidt was very popular with most of his teammates, perhaps in part because, after Ty Cobb, who had few friends on the roster, made a disparaging remark about his fighting abilities, the 200-pound catcher, who prided himself on feats of strength and courage—pounding spikes into cement bare-handed, wrestling a bear, or daring teammates to punch him hard in the stomach—challenged the outfielder and beat him badly. Not even Cobb could mess with the Boss. He clung to the game after leaving the Tigers, with playing or managing stints with the Providence Grays, Mobile Sea Gulls, Vernon Tigers, Memphis Chickasaws, Sioux City Indians, Tulsa Oilers, Fort Smith Twins, Atlanta Crackers, Springfield (Missouri) Midgets, Kalamazoo Celery Pickers, and Quincy (Illinois) Red Birds, effectively touring every level of minor league baseball from A to D. His final year in the game, at Quincy, was 1927. Afterward, and doubtless along the way, Schmidt had a troubled life that included bankruptcy and bouts of alcoholism. He died in Altus, Arkansas, in 1932 and was buried in an unmarked grave. In 1969, the Tigers arranged for the placement of a tombstone.

CARD DETAILS: Throwing pose, Sweet Caporal, 350 series, factory 30. One of two variants.

JAMES BENTLEY "CY" SEYMOUR

CY SEYMOUR was born in Albany, New York, in 1872, less than a decade after the end of the Civil War. He was a two-position star, as both a **center fielder** and a pitcher, though by the time this card was published, he had long given up a place on the mound. Seymour broke into the majors with the New York Giants (1896–1900), then spent two years with the Baltimore Orioles of the newly formed American League (1901–1902) before returning to the National League with Cincinnati (1902–1906), moving back to the **Giants** (1906–1910), and, after a hiatus, appearing in 39 games for the Boston Braves (1913). Across sixteen seasons, he posted a batting average of .303, topping out at a league-best .377 with the Reds in 1905. In that year, he led the National League in hits, slugging, total bases, doubles, triples, and RBI, as well. Not only did Seymour hit consistently, but he also hit for power, stroking 96 triples and 52 home runs in an era when both were unusual. Nor was he a slouch on the pitching mound. Between 1896 and 1900, he compiled a record of 61-56, with 105 complete games. Between 1897 and 1899, he pitched, on average, more than 300 innings per season, leading the league in walks three times and strikeouts twice. The effects of so much work on his arm doubtless led to his move to the outfield, where he had played sparingly already. He was not known as a great glove man, and in one notorious incident, in the playoff game that resulted from Fred Merkle's baserunning mistake in 1908, it was Seymour who lost a fly ball in the sun that led to three Cubs runs and the eventual loss of the pennant by the Giants. Seymour died in New York City in 1919.

CARD DETAILS: Duplicates. Both are throwing pose, Sweet Caporal, 350 series, factory 30. One of three variants.

WILLIAM PORTER "SPIKE" SHANNON

SPIKE SHANNON was born in Pittsburgh in 1875 and did not play his first major league game until he was 29 years old. From 1898 through 1903, this **left fielder** bounced around the minor leagues with stops at the Charleston (South Carolina) Seagulls of the Class B Southern League, the Richmond Bluebirds of the Class B Atlantic League, the Syracuse Stars of the Class A Eastern League, the Meriden Sil-verites of the Class F Connecticut State League, the Jersey City City (not a typo!) and Harrisburg Ponies of the then-unclassified Atlantic League, the Indianapolis/Matthews Hoosiers of the Class A Western Association, and the St. Paul Saints of the Western Association and then the American Association. Somehow, he had enough energy left to debut with the St. Louis Cardinals (1904–1906), then move on to the Giants (1906–1908) and the Pirates (1908) before joining the **Kansas City Blues** (1909–1911) of the Class A American Association, where the T206 cards found him. Shannon ended his career with the Virginia Ore Diggers of Virginia, Minnesota, in the Class C Northern League in 1913. During his five major league seasons, Shannon batted .259 in just under 700 at-bats, with 145 stolen bases, or 29 per year on average. He led the league in plate appearances in both 1906 and 1907. On defense, he was known for his spectacular catches in left field. When his playing days were behind him, Shannon turned to umpiring, first in the Northern League and then in the Federal League for both of its seasons, before moving to the Western League, the American Association, and the Southern Association. After 1931, he left the game for jobs with a golf practice range and a department store, both in Minneapolis. He died there in 1940.

CARD DETAILS: Sweet Caporal, 350 series, factory 30.

BAYARD HESTON "BUD" SHARPE

BUD SHARPE, born in West Chester, Pennsylvania, in 1881, was a graduate of Penn State College, where he led the baseball team as its captain and earned a degree in electrical engineering in 1903. He turned down an offer to teach mathematics at the school in favor of playing professional baseball and then had a brief and bifurcated major league career. A **first baseman** and right fielder, Sharpe played in 46 games for the Boston Beaneaters in 1905, and then in four games for the Pittsburgh Pirates and 115 for the Boston Doves in 1910. He was a .222 hitter and a decent fielder, though a standout in neither category. Between these two visits to "the show," Sharpe played for a year with the Scranton Miners (1906) of the Class B New York State League and for three seasons (1907–1909) with the **Newark** Sailors, and then **Indians** of the Class A Eastern League, which is where the T206 collection found him. He rounded out his career with the Buffalo Bisons of the Eastern League (1911) and the Oakland Oaks of the Class AA Pacific Coast League (1912). His year in Oakland, where he also managed the team, was statistically his best, with a batting average of .300 in 101 games. The 1912 Oaks team had a notable year as well, apparently compiling a record of 120-83 while anchored by a true iron man, twenty-six-year-old third baseman Gus Hetling, who played in 202 of those games and compiled a batting average of .297 in no less than 708 official at-bats. The winning record notwithstanding, the grind of such a season may have taken its toll. Sharpe's health took a turn for the worse, and in 1916, he died of tuberculosis in Haddock, Georgia, at the age of 34.

CARD DETAILS: Sweet Caporal, 350 series, factory 30. One of two variants.

GEORGE HENRY "HEINIE" SMITH

HEINIE SMITH was born in Pittsburgh in 1871, putting him among the oldest of the T206 players. He was a smallish **second baseman**, standing five-nine and weighing 160 pounds. His major league tenure included time with the Louisville Colonels (1897-1898), the Pittsburgh Pirates (1899), the New York Giants (1901–1902), and the Detroit Tigers (1903). Though he did bat .283 in 53 at-bats during his season with the Pirates, overall, he was a mediocre hitter with a career average of .237. His fielding average over these years of .935 was adequate but not stellar, though, in 1902, he led National League second basemen in putouts with 354. For a brief period that year, he also managed the Giants, who had a dismal record of 5-27 under his tutelage. In that role, Smith was succeeded by the soon-to-be legendary John McGraw. His years in the majors were punctuated with visits to the minor leagues, most notably with the Rochester Bronchos of the Class A Eastern League (1899, 1900–1901, and 1903), and he returned to Rochester (1904–1905) following his year with Detroit before moving on to the **Buffalo Bisons** (1906–1909, 1910), the Montreal Royals (1910), and the Newark Indians (1911), all again in the Eastern League. He closed out his career in Class B baseball, first with the Troy Trojans of the New York State League (1911) and later with the Erie Yankees of the Canadian League (1914). Smith died in Buffalo, New York, in 1939.

CARD DETAILS: Sweet Caporal, 350 series, factory 30.

JAMES WALTER "LITTLE NEMO" STEPHENS

STEPHENS, ST. LOUIS AMER.

JIM STEPHENS, who, for reasons that are lost to history, seems to have acquired his nickname from a comic strip character of the era, was born in Salineville, Ohio, in 1883. The five-foot-six, 157-pound **catcher** played for the **St. Louis Browns** for six years from 1907–1912. He was hardly a workhorse, never once playing in 100 games in a season, but he generally played in about half of the team's games each year. Across the six seasons, he compiled a batting average of .220 and a slugging percentage of .285. Perhaps because of his small size, it is fair to characterize him as a light hitter and not much of an offensive threat. Defensively, though, he had a particularly good year in 1910, when he led American League catchers in assists, double plays turned, and runners caught stealing. He continued in baseball for five seasons after leaving the Browns, including two years with the Class AA Buffalo Bisons of the International League (1913–1914), a year with the Dallas Giants of the Class B Texas League (1915), and two years with the Springfield (Massachusetts) Ponies of the Class B Eastern League (1916–1917). Little more is known of Stephens' life, including the specific circumstances that earned him his nickname. He died in Oxford, Alabama, in 1965.

CARD DETAILS: Sweet Caporal, 350 series, factory 30.

EDWARD FRANCIS SWEENEY

ED SWEENEY was born in Chicago in 1888. A six-one, 200-pound **catcher**, he spent most of his career in the majors with the **New York Highlanders**, or the Yankees as they were known from 1913 onward, of the American League (1908–1915), returning in 1919 for a brief one month stint with the Pittsburgh Pirates of the National League. He was an adequate hitter for his position, with a career batting average of .232 that trailed off markedly after 1913. But he was a solid hand behind the plate, leading American League catchers in putouts (1912), assists (1913), fewest errors (1909, 1912), fewest passed balls (1913), fewest stolen bases allowed (1913), and runners caught stealing (1912, 1913). Like so many other players, when his major league career had more or less ended, he stayed in the game by playing in the minors. But unlike so many others, his level of play was sustained. He spent two years with the Toledo Iron Men (1916–1917) of the American Association, part of a year with the Seattle Rainiers (1919) of the Pacific Coast League, and then a final season with the Kansas City Blues (1920) of the American Association, all at the Class AA level. Sweeney died in Chicago in 1947.

CARD DETAILS: Sweet Caporal, 350 series, factory 30.

WHAT'S IN TED'S WALLET? • 95

JESSE NILES "POWDER" TANNEHILL

JESSE TANNEHILL, born in Dayton, Kentucky, in 1874, had a life before baseball—as a saloon owner. Primarily a **pitcher** and a successful one, he also played in the outfield from time to time and even pinch-hit in 57 major league games. Tannehill played in the major leagues for fifteen seasons, with teams that included the Reds (1894), the Pirates (1897–1902), the New York Highlanders (1903), the Boston Americans/Red Sox (1904–1908), the **Washington Nationals** (1908–1909), and then back to "Go" with the Reds (1911). His seven years in the American League and his eight in the National League showed some remarkable consistencies, for example, in his number of strikeouts—470 in the former, 474 in the latter. His strikeout pitch was a slow curve. Overall, he pitched to an ERA of 2.80. He led the National League in ERA in 1901 with a mark of 2.18, which was not, in fact, his personal best; that came the following season at 1.95. In that same year, 1902, he pitched a total of 231 innings without yielding a single home run. He had superior control on the mound. A switch-hitter, he was also capable at the plate, with a career batting average of .255 (.277 during his years with the Pirates) and a slugging percentage of .337. Not too shabby for a little guy—only five foot eight and 150 pounds. After his playing career ended, he stayed involved in baseball, whether as a manager, an umpire, or a coach. Later, he worked in a Cincinnati machine shop. He died in Dayton, Kentucky, in 1956.

CARD DETAILS: Sweet Caporal, 350 series, factory 30.

Luther Haden "Dummy" Taylor

The Deadball Era was not known for its cultural sensitivity. DUMMY TAYLOR, so nicknamed because he was deaf, was born in Oskaloosa, Kansas, in 1875. A right-handed **pitcher**, he played for the New York Giants from 1900–1908, interrupted only briefly by a four-game run with the Cleveland Blues (1902). He finished his career with a winning record of 116-106 and an ERA of 2.75. In 1901, he pitched a remarkable 353 innings for the Giants and posted a record of 18-27 while leading the league in hits allowed, which may explain why they dispatched him, briefly, to Cleveland at the start of the following season. Still, he managed to pitch more than 200 innings every year from then through 1906, and in eight of his major league seasons, his yearly ERA was below his career figure. After the 1908 season with the Giants, he moved on to the **Buffalo Bisons** (1909–1911) and then the Montreal Royals (1911–1912) of the Class A Eastern League, the Montgomery Rebels (1913) and the New Orleans Pelicans (1913) of the Class A Southern Association, the Brantford (Ontario) Red Sox of the Class B Canadian League (1914), and the Utica Utes of the Class B New York State League. In May 1902, Dummy Taylor took the mound against the Cincinnati Reds on the first Opening Day in their new ballpark. Leading off and playing center field for the Reds was William Ellsworth "Dummy" Hoy, beginning his final year with the team. This was the first and only time in Major League history when two deaf players competed against one another.[6] Dummy Taylor died in Jacksonville, Illinois, in 1958.

CARD DETAILS: Sweet Caporal, 350 series, factory 30.

---

6. See James Goodwin and Randy Fisher, "The 100th Anniversary of 'Dummy vs. Dummy,' Society for American Baseball Research, November 26, 2003, found online March 22, 2024, at https://sabr.org/journal/article/the-100th-anniversary-of-dummy-vs-dummy/.

IRA FELIX THOMAS

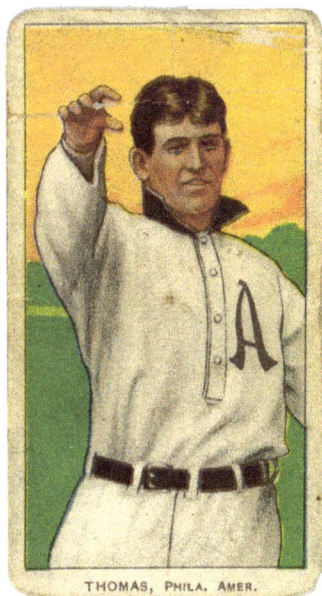

THOMAS, PHILA. AMER.

IRA THOMAS was born in Ballston Spa, New York, also the birthplace of the supposed inventor of baseball, Abner Doubleday, in 1881. After two seasons with the New York Highlanders (1906–1907) and a third with the Detroit Tigers (1908), where he was platooned against left-handed pitching, Thomas had developed a reputation as a weak-armed defender. But in the seven seasons that followed, with Connie Mack's **Philadelphia Athletics** (1909–1915), he prospered, at least on defense. In 1909, he had the best fielding percentage of any American League **catcher**. He was a career .242 hitter, though he hit nine points higher during his years with the A's. But in ten games across three World Series (1908, 1910, 1911), he batted only .214. Indeed, though he was with the A's for the 1913 and 1914 postseasons, he did not play an inning, despite Mack's having designated him as team captain in 1914. And when his playing days were over, Thomas did not follow the well-worn path to the minors. Off the field, he had differences with some teammates and others over nascent efforts at forming a players' union, on which question he eventually sided with management. He left the professional game for a time, first to coach the Williams College baseball team and later to invest in an oil field venture, returning in 1923–1924 to manage the A's affiliate in Shreveport, the Gassers, of which he was the lead owner for a time. Thomas then stayed in baseball as a scout and occasional coach. He died in Philadelphia in 1958.

CARD DETAILS: Sweet Caporal, 350 series, factory 30.

ROBERT ALEXANDER UNGLAUB

UNGLAUB, WASHINGTON

BOB UNGLAUB was born in Baltimore, Maryland, in 1880 and graduated in 1903 from Maryland Agricultural College, known today as the University of Maryland. A **utility infielder** who played in the minor leagues while attending school, with stops including the Petersburg Farmers in the Class B Virginia League (1895—at age 15), the Worcester Farmers in the Class A Eastern League (1900, 1901), the Meriden Silverites of the Class F Connecticut State League (1900), the Sacramento Gilt Edges of the independent California League (1902), and the Milwaukee Brewers of the Class A American Association (1903). He broke into the majors with the New York Highlanders (1904), then moved to the Boston Americans/Red Sox (1904–1907), finally landing with the **Washington Nationals** (1908–1910) before beginning a downward slide through the minor league ranks until he played his final three seasons with the Fargo-Morehead Graingrowers (1914–1916) of the Class C Northern League. Through it all, he was, at best, a journeyman player who left but a small impression on the game. His major league batting average of .258 was respectable, as was his fielding, but he never stood out for his performance in any single season. Where he did stand out, however, was in his seemingly continuous arguments over his salary, including at least one appeal that went all the way to the National Commission. He also had a moralistic streak that, on one occasion, saw him proclaiming his shame at being a baseball player, a profession he found degrading and sinful, filled with reprobates. On balance, Bob Unglaub was not a well-liked player. He died in Baltimore in 1916.

CARD DETAILS: Sweet Caporal, 350 series, factory 30.

ROBERT EDGAR "FARMER" WILLETT

WILLETTS, DETROIT

FARMER WILLETT was born in Norfolk, Virginia, in 1884. His mother, a teacher and writer, was a descendant of Samuel Adams. After playing for two years with the Wichita Jobbers of the Class C Western Association (1905–1906), he joined the **pitching** staff of the **Detroit Tigers**, where, never a star, he nevertheless became a mainstay from 1906–1913. His best year was 1909, when he posted a record of 21-10, pitching 25 complete games and a total of 292 innings pitched. Over his ten-year career with Detroit, Willett went 102-100 with an ERA of 3.08. Though the team was in the World Series each year from 1907–1909, Willett pitched in only two games in 1909, giving up one run over seven-plus innings of work. As a fellow Southerner who joined the Tigers at about the same time, Willett was the only member of the team willing to room the young Ty Cobb both at home and on the road. But apparently, Willett was pressured by others on the team to move out and leave Cobb on his own, which he did, earning Cobb's enduring enmity. Willett tended to pitch inside and was always willing to defend his teammates, which led to a number of hit batters, a category in which he led the American League in 1912. Willett ended his career in the majors after jumping to the St. Louis Terriers of the Federal League for the 1914 and 1915 seasons. He then played in the minor leagues until 1919. After retiring, he ran a pool hall for a time and worked as a carpenter. He died in Wellington, Kansas, in 1934.

CARD DETAILS: Sweet Caporal, 350 series, factory 30. One of two variants. This card misspells the player's last name.

VICTOR GAZAWAY WILLIS

WILLIS, PITTSBURG

VIC WILLIS was born in Cecil County, Maryland, in 1876. He attended the University of Delaware for one year before entering the ranks of professional baseball players. A rangy, six-two right-handed **pitcher**, he spent eight seasons with the Boston Beaneaters of the National League (1898–1905), then four with the **Pirates** (1906–1909), before ending his major league career in St. Louis (1910). His career record of 249-205 and ERA of 2.63, along with 1651 strikeouts over nearly 4000 innings pitched, earned him a place in the Hall of Fame. Recognized as the National League's pitcher of the year in 1899, he led the league in strikeouts in 1902, in shutouts twice (1899, 1901), and in complete games twice (1902, 1904). In the 1902 season, Willis pitched 410 innings, the second-highest total in modern National League history, and recorded 45 complete games, the most of any pitcher in the modern (post-1900) era. He pitched in only two World Series games in 1909 against Detroit, striking out three, walking eight, and taking one loss. In 1901, when the American League began its challenge to the National for major league status—the challenge that eventually led to the National Agreement two years later—Willis threatened to jump to the new league but then backed down. In 1909, Willis was chosen to pitch in the grand opening game of Forbes Field; his four-hitter was not enough for the win against the Cubs. In retirement, Willis purchased and operated the Washington House Hotel in Newark, Delaware. He died in Elkton, Maryland, in 1947.

CARD DETAILS: Pittsburg, Sweet Caporal, 350 series, factory 30. One of three variants.

Concluding Thoughts

AMERICA IN 1909 was near the fulcrum point of its transition from a predominantly agrarian society with a nineteenth-century-style industrial sector and from a strictly continental power with, at best, a modest role in international affairs characterized more by its potentialities than its accomplishments into a predominantly urban society, a highly innovative and rapidly expanding twentieth-century industrial economy, and a global power with imperial aspirations—from an afterthought in world affairs to a centerpiece. Through his inventions, Thomas Edison, by many lights the leading innovator of his time, was among the most significant engineers of that transition. And as professional baseball matured during those same years, developing its own modern infrastructure and iconography, it emerged as one of the essential unifying forces of the era, a shared cultural experience around which the diverse parts of the newly modern nation could come together.

In that sense, in that era, baseball truly was the National Pastime, one that was encapsulated, as in a single still photograph, by the series of T206 baseball cards issued in 1909 through 1911 by the American Tobacco Company.

In their day, the cards in Ted's Wallet likely provided a bond between father and son, between a self-acknowledged lifelong fan of sixty-two years and his youngest son of just twelve, growing to love the game in his own right, and between Ted and his schoolmates as well. Today, more than a century later, when the country is an extraordinary amalgam of allied and competing interests, when the game is no longer pastoral in any sense of the word, and when the larger world sometimes seems chaotic beyond comprehension, let alone control, the enduring appeal

The Edison Family: Charles, Mina, Thomas, Madeleine, and Theodore [1]

of these cards may well lie in the reminder they represent of the sheer beauty of a simpler game in simpler times. Continuity. Connectivity. Perhaps even Comfort.

What's in Ted's Wallet?

Maybe just that.

---

1. This photograph, with Ted at the far right, his face partially obscured by a flaw in developing, is in the archive of the Thomas Edison National Historical Park, found online March 23, 2024, at https://npgallery.nps.gov/AssetDetail/50c0e87e138c4184a81d57522fda32d9.

Acknowledgments

EXCEPT WHERE otherwise noted, the images used, including the photograph on the cover and the T206 cards themselves, as well as the other materials referenced in this book, are found in the archives of the Thomas Edison National Historical Park (TENHP) in West Orange, New Jersey. The TENHP encompasses both the Original Edison Works laboratory complex and the Edisons' nearby estate, Glenmont. The authors are grateful to the Park staff for their assistance in preparing this book, and especially to Archivist Leonard DeGraaf and Museum Technician Valerie Shoffner, without whose suggestions and support this project could not exist.

The brief player biographies featured on pages 42 to 100, though not fully annotated, draw upon many sources. Primary among these are the roster of players featured on the T206 cards published by the T206 Museum, the player biographies published by the Society for American Baseball Research, of which both authors are members, and the statistical profiles found on the *Baseball Almanac* and *Baseball Reference* websites. These are key resources for anyone interested in baseball history, and the authors gratefully acknowledge their valuable contribution to this book.

Finally, we are grateful to the professionals of the Sunbury Press team, and especially to Katie Cressman, Crystal Devine, and John Jordan, whose efforts have contributed meaningfully to the volume you have before you. Thank you.

About the Authors

J B MANHEIM is Professor Emeritus at The George Washington University, where he developed the world's first degree-granting program in political communication and was later founding director of the School of Media & Public Affairs. In 1995 he was named Professor of the Year for the District of Columbia. He learned his love of baseball watching Dizzy Dean on the Game of the Week and huddling with his grandfather for warmth on July nights at The Mistake By The Lake, AKA, Cleveland Municipal Stadium, and renewed it when the National Pastime finally returned to the Nation's Capital. He is a member of SABR (Society for American Baseball Research) and the Internet Baseball Writers Association of America.

LAWRENCE KNORR is a lifelong baseball fan and member of SABR. He has written or co-authored several baseball books and numerous other histories and biographies. Lawrence graduated from Wilson College with a BA in Business and Economics with a minor in History. He earned an MBA from Penn State, focusing on finance and operations. He has completed all course work and comprehensive exams at Liberty University and is now working on his dissertation required for a Ph.D. in History. Lawrence has had a long career in information technology and has been an entrepreneur and executive. He is the founder and CEO of Sunbury Press, Inc., the trade publisher. You can listen to Lawrence's podcast, *The Sunbury Press Books Show* on the BookSpeak Network.

www.ingramcontent.com/pod-product-compliance
Lightning Source LLC
Chambersburg PA
CBHW051209090426
42740CB00021B/3435